Nyeri
Mara
Narok
Musoma
MARA
Magadi
Lake Natron
Athi
Tsavo
Galana
Malindi
Voi
Kilimanjaro
Moshi
Arusha
Lake Eyasi
Lake Manyara
Nyumba ya Mungu Dam
Pangani
KILIMANJARO
Shinyanga
Nzega
ARUSHA
Mombasa
Wembere
Singida
Kondoa
Pemba
Tanga
Wete
Korogwe
Pangani
Mkoani
TANGA
Mkokotoni
DODOMA
Dodoma
SINGIDA
Zanzibar
Koani
Wami
Kibaha
DAR ES SALAAM
Dar es Salaam
Kilosa
Morogoro
Njombe
Kisigo
Great
PWANI
INDIAN
Ruaha
Ruaha
Mafia Island
Iringa
Rufiji
Kilindoni
BEYA
Great
IRINGA
Ifakara
OCEAN
Kilombero
Kilwe Kivinje
Mbeya
Luwegu
MOROGORO
Tukuyu
Njombe
LINDI
Chitipa
Mbwemburu
Karonga
Lindi
Mtwara
Lake Nyasa
Songea
Masasi
RUVUMA
MTWARA
Tunduru
Ruvuma
Ruvuma
Mzuzu
Nkhata Bay
Rio Rovuma
Mueda

# C'est l'Afrique
# That's Africa

*'Allah il Allah il hamdu lillahi'*
*Allah stood by us! Anno Hecker with an elephant*
*(Tanganyika, 15 October 1958)*

# C'est l' Afrique
# That's Africa

A Somewhat Different Hunting Book

By Anno Hecker

Rowland Ward Publications
Johannesburg

ISBN 978-0-9802626-2-9

C'est l'Afrique – That's Africa © Anno Hecker 2007

First English Edition August 2007
(German Edition 2003)

Rowland Ward Publications
P O Box 2079, Houghton 2041 South Africa
Tel: (27 11) 646 0781
email: sales@rowlandward.com
or
P O Box 1222
Spotsylvania, VA 22553 USA
Tel: (877) 424 3220
email: RowlandWard@wwdb.org

www.rowlandward.com

All rights reserved. No part of this publication
may be reproduced in any form whatsoever
without the prior permission of the publishers.

Photographic credits
Gronefeld, Gerhard: cover photograph, pp 34, 35, 39
Rakow, Frank: pp 72, 90, 101
Stronarch, Brian: pp 23, 136

Edited by Brian Marsh
Design and reproduction, Collage Graphics
Lithographed and bound, PaarlPrint

*Ye who have travelled the Wilderness,*
*ye who have followed the chase, whom the voice*
*of the forest comforts, and the touch of the lonely place;*
*Ye who are sib to the Jungle and*
*know it and hold it good – praise ye the name*
*of Nimrod, a fellow who understood.*
*(H.B. of Punch, in his Ode to*
*the Followers of Nimrod)*

# Contents

*Pat Hemingway with Anno Hecker in 1964*
*To the left is the author's son, Ernst*

# INTRODUCTION

Patrick Hemingway, son of the famous writer, Ernest Hemingway, told me that when he was fifteen years old, he was keen on following in his famous father's footsteps and he submitted a five page essay to his father for assessment. "Not so bad," commented the old man after scrutinizing the script, "but on only two pages it would have been better." This is the advice I have tried to follow when writing these lines, although occasionally I have been tempted to lose myself in detail.

For a long time I have resisted requests from family and friends to publish some of my African experiences before I became an 'armchair hunter', as Americans so aptly call old and inactive sportsmen, in order to reveal some of my memories (covering almost half a century) and to give some idea of what the African wilderness and its people were like.

I must warn the reader not to expect dozens of tracked and shot man-eaters or scores of one hundred pounds aside elephant, as I have not been one of those lucky fellows who were born and bred in Kenya with the opportunity to hunt big game from their childhood onwards. From notes and my memory I have written, in no particular order, what I consider important and of interest to sportsmen. I have deliberately abstained from giving any advice on modern, wildlife management and, instead, I have recounted some adventures of early colonial hunters that might be of interest to the modern hunter.

Had I written this book 20 years ago, it would have contained more stories of successful stalks and sensational bags which may have pleased the young adventurous nimrod as well as the trophy freak whose measuring tape sits as loose as his trigger-finger. I have to admit that I too definitely admired a good or rare pair of horns, or a trophy I had to work very hard to get, although nowadays, less out of a wish to boast about them but more as a memory of the past; they call back the atmosphere of the bush and supply me, from time to time, with the shadowy apparition of dear and well known faces – black, brown and white – which show up for a few seconds before fading away. Faces of friends, trackers and bearers, most of whom passed away many years ago.

As an official thank you for my time in the Foreign Aid Service, I still have a letter from the Permanent Secretary acknowledging my "outstanding services rendered to the Federal Republic of Germany". Surely a noble gesture but admittedly not as much appreciated as the words of an old, illiterate tracker from the Luwegu river in the Selous.

In the 1980s, when a friend had wounded an elephant, I asked our professional hunter, a Maasai, whether he would allow me to finish off the wounded beast which had gone into the thick stuff. The Maasai handed over his .458 FN Mauser with pleasure for the *coup de grâce*. On entering the thicket, Mfupa, the withered old tracker, wanted to guide me, an offer I kindly declined as I preferred to go alone on probably the last elephant hunt of my life. Whereupon Mfupa, with a respectful look in his eyes, remarked in Kiswaheli, "Ah! This one is still one of the old hunters from very long ago."

Anno Hecker
2003

# Foreword

But for a short interruption in 1962, the author served as field officer, tsetse control officer, elephant control officer and the first German project leader and instructor at the Game Warden Training Centre, College of African Wildlife Management (CAWM), in Tanzania. He was an honorary game warden of Tanganyika, Tanzania and Kenya and, after his return to Europe, he served as a forester and game warden for 23 years in a state forest in the Eifel, Rhineland, which was home to red deer, roe deer, wild boar and moufflon.

Since 1963, he has been an official measurer for Rowland Ward's *Records of Big Game* and, from 1970 to 2002, he hunted annually on four to five week safaris in East, West and South Africa, either for himself or to accompany and guide friends on big game hunts. Anno Hecker's memories cover an important part of the history of African hunting and are based on experiences that would be a pity to lose. Christopher Borthen, editor of the *British Stalking* magazine, once said, "A day with Mr Hecker is equal to a whole year in Africa."

Some years ago we visited Europe's biggest game fair, *Jagd und Hund*, in Dortmund, Germany, where at the stand of Safari Willscher there happened to be Mr Muhichia Ndolanga, director of Tanzania Wildlife, who called out when he saw Anno, "This man knows more about big game and African hunting than anybody else at the whole exhibition!"

The old man's reply was, "How good it is that hardly anybody here understands English!" What a stroke of luck that eventually it was possible to break down his reserve. His last statement was, "The shadows grow longer ..."

Klaus Freund
(Prominent German sportsman)

*Foot safari – uncommon in recent times*

# PREFACE

In 1938, a wealthy uncle gave me and my eldest brother entrance tickets for a 'Nature' cinema show entitled, *Longing for Africa*, at the Ufa Palace in Cologne. As it was a long time before TV and wild animal magazines were unknown, fantastic movies of lions and elephants in the wild fired the imagination of a 10-year-old boy doomed to grow up in a city.

When the curtain fell, the film-maker stepped onto the podium to thank the audience for their interest and asked questioners to come forward. Only my brother and I took advantage of the invitation. We went forward with pounding hearts because we knew that the man waiting to talk to us was no less a person than Bengt Berg, the famous Swedish big game hunter, photographer and explorer whose well-illustrated books, translated into many languages, dominated as bestsellers in the bookstalls. I still remember the tall, lean man, with almost shy modesty, bowing down to shake hands with the 10-year-old boy and asking how he liked the film.

A year later, World War II suppressed all my wanderlust. At the age of 15, I was called up and drafted into an anti-aircraft regiment and served for 16 months as a gunner on an 88mm gun and endured the bombing and firestorms of Cologne, a time that I, a born pessimist, never expected to survive. What followed were the deprivations of the post-war years without any prospect for the future. So I took the advice of a professor in Bonn whom I had consulted about the possibility of studying Zoology, and who told me to become a bricklayer. With no time in those days to even think about the Great Wide World, my desired future was seemingly closed forever. But my situation was about to change sooner than I anticipated.

*Miles and miles of bloody Africa*

## Chapter One

# AFRICA!
## NAIROBI, NOVEMBER 1955

Purple blossoming Jacaranda avenues rushed towards us as we landed 22 hours after our departure from dreary, misty Frankfurt (via Athens, Cairo and Khartoum), in a four engined, propeller-driven plane, in those days the fastest possible connection.

My wife and I, in youthful euphoria, were overwhelmed by the confusing multitude of entirely new impressions and feelings: the variety of strange scents under a hot, gleaming sun; the unusual sight of crowds of surging Africans and Indians in the streets; and the disorderly traffic with the conspicuous safari cars of white hunters covered in red dust. At nearly every street corner there were armed, black policemen whose purpose we fortunately did not understand, not knowing that, only a few blocks further on, the last trial against the Field Marshal of the Mau Mau was being heard and whose tragic fight for freedom, based on the darkest superstitions, had cost over 13 000 lives.

How contrary the noble atmosphere in the hotels with their crowd of well-dressed waiters gliding silently across thick carpets, red fezzes on their frizzy heads, the guests in obligatory dinner jackets or evening dresses. And for us post-war Germans, the unfamiliar richness of the dishes. Then the almost ceremonial business the next day of being fitted out with made-to-measure safari apparel at Ahamed Brothers, the Indian tailors who would have everything ready the following morning.

Then, finally, the collection of our Land Rover for the trip via Arusha, Kondoa, Dodoma, Iringa and to our destination, the Southern Highlands of Tanganyika. Three days of driving over corrugated, earth roads with their numerous potholes was a real, physical stress, especially as the dust clouds behind the trucks we encountered made overtaking very risky. One could hardly cast one's eyes across the strange and unknown landscapes to the left or right and I quickly developed an understanding of the common English expression MMBA – miles and miles of bloody Africa.

My destination was 60 miles to the south of Iringa where I was going to manage the planting of a 2600 hectare wasteland with eucalyptus trees and South American pines on behalf of the Austrian owner, a task I tackled with understandable enthusiasm although, right at the beginning, a well-meaning and friendly neighbour advised me not to rush. "Hold your horses," he said. "You are in Africa. Forget what you learned at home and use your common sense!"

Step by step our then incomplete farmhouse became habitable. There was no electricity so we had to get used to the light of paraffin lamps. We took on local Africans for the kitchen, garden and for bringing the water we needed, which had to be carried up to the house in four-gallon tins. Then, just as we began to settle down, like a bolt from the blue, we had a visit from a government official who gave us the shattering news that, due to unsettled mortgages, the sale of the farm was invalid and the transfer to my employer void!

After the first shock we sent a mass of telegrams – there were no phones in those days – to Austria, Bonn, Dar-es-Salaam and Nairobi. But all efforts to rectify the affair were in vain, even the bringing in of Chancellor Adenauer failed, which I now know was for political reasons. Hell, what a mess and it seemed that our only option was to return, full of remorse, with our tails between our legs, to Germany. The words of the chief forester for North-Rhine Westphalia when handing over my exam certificate were still ringing in my ears: "And the best of luck to you in German East Africa." The big boss had been a staunch admirer of General von Lettow-Vorbeck.

I was not born with a silver, nor even a green, spoon in my mouth. There were no sportsmen among my lower middle-class forefathers. Before my hard-won admittance to the forestry profession, the remark was often heard "you lack the green tradition", meaning there had been no foresters in our family.

But to return to Germany was not an option for me. I had to stay in that wonderful country and it was just a question of how to achieve it. I applied for a job in the forestry and game departments and approached the larger farm owners but everywhere I was met with polite refusals – were there still feelings of resentment against Germany so shortly after the war?

Then the breakthrough, the decisive tip, the tsetse department had vacancies for field officers but hardly anybody applied as nobody wanted to put up with the strain of working in swamps and sleeping-sickness areas to tackle the deadly insects. So I applied and got a job as a field officer, which turned out to be the greatest time of my life!

*Old buffalo, Mara, Kenya 1987*

## Chapter Two

# BUFFALO
## A HUNTER'S BEGINNING

The year was 1955 and the very first large animal I saw after my arrival was a big, male kudu. It almost ran into me as it crossed the road while I was on my way to the Southern Highlands. In the harsh light of high noon it seemed almost greyish-blue in appearance. Given their scarcity at the time, the sighting was a privilege granted to only a few East Africans during the course of a lifetime – an experience that was instrumental in expanding my enthusiasm for this unique and proud animal. But due to my inexperience, being completely on my own, without an armed companion, with scanty Kiswaheli (the lingua franca of East Africa) and also being advised that my 9.3x62 Mauser was possibly too light a rifle for such formidable game, it is perhaps understandable that I reacted somewhat over-cautiously and did not follow the bull.

Towards the end of my time in Africa, I often stalked on my own without a tracker and relied on my trusty .458. It was during these hunts that I bagged some of my biggest trophies. Even today, after such a long period of time, I can still feel the almost unbearable tension of those first safaris when following fresh tracks of a solitary, old bull, for example, leading from a waterhole into the bush.

For the greenhorn who, up to then, had never seen a Cape buffalo, neither in the wild nor in a zoo, my first hunt for them was incredibly exciting. The large hoof-print was round, almost 15 centimetres in diameter, with a narrow shadow falling across the spoor caused by the rising sun. There were no dried grass stalks or leaves in the imprint as the wind had yet to come up. Our footsteps sounded much too loud for my ears. The wind started to circle when the sun rose higher, which made me even more nervous. We were in thick bush, the buffalo's droppings still warm and the field of view from 10 to 15 metres at the most. The butt of the rifle in my right hand

*A young hunter with a young buffalo 1956...*

was wet from sweat although the heat of the day was not yet perceptible.

Suddenly, the tracker, whose loincloth was his only garment, dropped down on one knee. There was absolute silence, no chirping of birds or cicadas. I only heard the pounding of my heart and felt the flow of blood in my ears while I tried to detect something in the confusion of dry grass and interwoven tendrils. Before I realized what was happening, a dark shape rose out of the entangled matter and grew taller and taller. My God, I thought, no buffalo can possibly be that big! I saw a slate-grey horn behind the vegetation and an ear with frayed edges twitching nervously forward. Then I saw the malicious stare for which Robert Ruark formulated the oft-quoted phrase: "He looks at you as if you owe him money". And then, with an explosive snort, a breaking of branches and a whirling of dust, the show was over. My eyes still focussed on the empty space, still searching for a vital spot that had just vanished ... It is unbelievable how fast and agile these black giants are.

*...and an old hunter with an old buffalo 1988*

*I never imagined that lions could kill buffalo bulls...*

For newcomers, these old, solitary, bull buffalo possibly represent the best start into big game hunting. Pushed out of the breeding herd at the age of 10 or 12 years old by younger and more virile bulls, they are forced to follow a different feeding pattern due to their worn teeth. They lose the protection of the group and become prone to predation by lions, especially as their strength, agility and senses of hearing and smell deteriorate. So they often congregate in smaller or larger 'bachelor clubs', the size of which depends on the local buffalo population. On the Moyowasi, in western Tanzania, I once counted 53 males in one such group with some really big bulls among them.

On the other hand, I remember a very old bull on the Usangu Flats, in southern Tanzania, that was on his own except for a younger askari (as they are called in the hunting field), as his bodyguard. The trophies from these old bulls consist mainly of the bosses as the horns have usually been worn down and, when finally I shot the old bull in question, I was a bit disappointed as its bosses lacked the heaviness I had expected.

A common sight in East Africa were the vultures. Often falling down like stones from a dizzy height after discovering dying game, or perching in great numbers in the trees, which usually indicated a lion kill. When gliding around a certain spot in wide circles, they shortened some otherwise rather difficult searches for wounded

*A very old bull with ox-peckers on its back*

game. On one of my first safaris, which was not very successful due to inexperience, the locally engaged Africans who tracked for me advised me to shoot a vulture as the skull of a scavenger put under the pillow at night would reveal where to find buffalo the following morning. This, of course, I refused to do as vultures were protected. Even nowadays, a widespread superstition endangers vultures in Africa as their skulls are coveted 'charms' of the witchdoctors and are much in demand by punters when betting on the horses.

It was due to vultures sitting in a far away, prominent fig tree, that I was able to take one of my best buffalo. Instead of finding a lion kill when we carefully approached the tree, we found a huge buffalo in a waterhole that was still very much alive despite having been severely mauled. There must have been a Battle Royal and I wondered what had happened to the lion or lions. The vultures, of course, were waiting to see if the injured beast was going to die or not.

When I began hunting, I never imagined that lions could kill buffalo bulls as these can weigh up to 800 kilograms. The highest authentic weight so far on record was from a bull shot at Lake Rukwa, in Tanzania, which weighed 918.2 kilograms. It had atrophied testicles, the result no doubt of an early castration inflicted by a predator. It had narrow, almost cow-like bosses, while its spread amounted to 53 inches. The bull was shot in 1964 by a game warden, a very successful, renowned hunter and a specialist in

*Shoulder shot – no problem with a solid*

hunting down man-eaters who guided Marshal Tito and Prince Bernhard of the Netherlands on the orders of the Government.

The heaviest bull scaled by the CAWM was 772 kilograms and the average weight of eight, full grown bulls from Lake Victoria, an area famous for large-bodied buffalo, averaged 756 kilograms. Estimated weights of over a ton are mostly the fantasy of tyro hunters and, of course, my first buffalo weighed 'a ton' as well!

Many lion kills that we found convinced me of the extraordinary strength lions must have to master full-grown buffalo bulls. The skulls lying beside many of the skeletons would have been the pride of many a trophy hunter.

Reports of charging buffalo are legendary and belong to the repertoire of any greenhorn or newcomer but they are certainly not always 'huntsman's yarns'. It does happen quite often though that the shot animal, not knowing what has happened, accidentally runs towards the hunter to reach cover. But when following a wounded buffalo, the hunter often unconsciously gets too close due to thick vegetation and comes within the bull's 'circle of instantaneous attack', when it will always charge.

Nobody who has not experienced this happening can imagine how suddenly a wounded buffalo explodes out of cover. Without any doubt, at that very moment, the stopping power of a bullet weighing

*In the thick stuff*

500-grains or more is the best medicine provided one hits the beast with immediate crippling effect and that is important. While the other members of the Big Five can usually be turned by a less deadly hit, a buffalo, once having made up its mind, cannot be turned!

I have not experienced buffalo charging purposefully right after being hit, nor attacks by unwounded animals, not even cows with very young calves. Normally they are peaceful beasts but one can be charged by unprovoked animals suffering from old wounds as happened to me twice. Both carried festering sores from muzzle-loaders.

For a frontal chest shot you have to rely on a solid bullet but, on broadside shots, heavy calibre, soft-nose bullets are recommended to avoid the missile exiting and wounding other animals standing behind.

One late afternoon, some years ago, while hunting with a friend in the Caprivi Strip, in Namibia, he shot a facing bull right in the centre of the chest with a soft-nose bullet from his Winchester .375 H&H Magnum. Only late the next morning was the wounded animal found and finished. His 300-grain bullet had disintegrated before reaching the vitals while a solid bullet would have saved us from a long search and the poor animal from a lot of pain.

If the herd bull has been shot and cleanly put down and the herd does not know where the danger lies, the whole lot may stampede in a compact mass towards you – not charging but fleeing downwind. I have experienced such a stampede three times and it was hard to keep cool. These are truly fearful moments. The ground trembles from the thundering hoof beats of the herd and you can be excused for jumping up and down, gun at the ready and screaming at the top of your voice to try to make the herd split. There can be nothing worse than to turn and run away at these times as you can easily be run over.

I knew a famous, Danish, white hunter who would never tackle a herd with his clients. Certainly more hunters have been killed by buffalo than by any other big game. The search for wounded buffalo is a chapter of its own and becomes a special problem when a slightly wounded bull has joined a herd overnight or, when in thick stuff, the wrong animal is shot.

But worse than the buffalo itself, can be an unreliable member within the hunting group who loses control of his nerves and fires his weapon in an uncontrolled manner. Whenever I see four or more armed men following buffalo spoor on videos, I get goose-pimples.

Attacks occur mostly from short distances, out of thick vegetation

*Abnormal buffalo cow*

and always heralded by a loud and nerve-racking snort. Mostly there is time for just one shot that should not be fired when panic-stricken. The bull comes with his head up, otherwise he could not see, and lowers it at the last moment to toss his adversary. A wounded bull can take a lot of killing. A friend of mine finally killed his bull in the Kitete swamp in the Rift Valley only after the 18th shot from his 9.3x62 calibre rifle.

I would like to mention some noteworthy buffalo attacks from old times in order to save them from oblivion. When still a lad, in 1845, Oom Paul Kruger owed his life to his outstanding strength. When he was attacked by an enraged buffalo cow, he managed to get hold of its horns and press its head into the mud of the waterhole he was in, blinding it with mud and almost suffocating it.

Paul Graetz, known for crossing Africa in a motor car in 1907, got away less lightly. Four years later, in Southern Rhodesia, he wounded a buffalo bull with several near-vital shots from his 9.3x62

*Now its the seconds that count ...*

rifle. During the follow-up, the beast charged, killed the French cameraman of the expedition and then injured Graetz so badly that he wrestled with death in a primitive bush hospital for weeks.

The famous hunter and naturalist, F.C. Selous, once felt the power of a charging buffalo when a wounded bull tossed his horse into the air "like a dog". That was at a time when buffalo still occurred in South Africa outside tsetse areas and could be chased on horseback, which was also a popular way to hunt elephants and lions.

A report in the second edition of the famous Brehms Tierleben, from 1879, is in several respects quite characteristic of a buffalo attack. I quote part of what he wrote: "... as it is known, one of our Africa travellers, Baron Harnier, also died in 1861 in a similar way. After he had wounded a buffalo the outraged animal tossed his native companion to the ground. To free the man lying underneath the horns Harnier attacked the buffalo with the butt of his rifle, thereby causing the beast to charge him. Harnier was found stamped into an unrecognisable mess; while the native far from helping his master to whom he owed his life ran away abandoning our worthy compatriot to his fate."

But perhaps the most tragic end to a buffalo hunt took place in 1970, in Northern Kenya, when the well-known professional hunter, Douglas Collins, was quite unexpectedly attacked in thick bush from a distance of only three metres. He just had time to fire both barrels of his double .470 into the buffalo before it knocked him over and gored and trampled him with its horns and hooves. His younger brother, Edward, who was visiting from England, fired his .30-06 at the bull and temporarily diverted it. This allowed Douglas to grasp his rifle lying nearby and reload it before the buffalo stood over him again. He fired both barrels from underneath it, the muzzle almost touching the buffalo's chest. One of the solid bullets exited the buffalo's body and hit his brother in the heart.

In thick bush I used to load solid bullets only. Right at the beginning of my hunting career I shot a bull half-facing towards me with a so-called 'strong jacketed' 9.3x62 bullet, which did not penetrate. Fortunately, I eventually managed to finish off the beast.

A friend of mine named Willy was being guided by Deniy Zaphiro, a well-known Kenyan game warden. After several days of hard hunting they found the buffalo of all hunters' dreams, with a 50-inch plus spread, high up on Mount Kenya. It was lying down half-facing them.

*Pat with his two best buffalo, 1956*

The hunters waited for the bull to rise but, when the wind began to veer with the rising sun, they became nervous that it would get their scent. Willy fired at it with his .458. What they saw, however, was splinters of horn flying through the air, whereupon the buffalo was up and gone before Willy could reload. "I'll bet you used a soft-nose," was my comment which, of course, he admitted was true.

Today, after so many years, it still upsets me tremendously to remember that I lost what would have been my biggest buffalo after a dramatic hunt on Mount Meru. During a drive one afternoon for buffalo raiding a pyrethrum field, I wounded a fast running bull. Pat Hemingway was with me and we followed the tracks without my tracker who, for reasons I have forgotten, was suddenly not available. That huge trophy bull repeatedly stopped in densest cover but he always got away without us being able to shoot. How we cursed that he would not charge us!

But then, when we were about to give up following because of impending darkness, it happened. The bull was lying behind a big tree under the ridge of a hill and it charged Pat, who was walking in front of me, from a distance of no more than two metres and knocked him down. At the same time, the bull hit a tree with the end of his right horn with such force that he slithered sideways, turned and disappeared at the speed of light over the ridge.

It was one of those very rare occasions when a buffalo broke off its charge. Standing a little lower than Pat, I had just fractions of a

*My last buffalo – and possibly my best*

second to quickly lift the muzzle of my .458, but to fire would have endangered my friend. Out of the corner of my eye, I thought I glimpsed the sling of Pat's .375 Winchester become entangled in the curve of the buff's horn. After the charge we sat down with wobbling knees to recover before we looked for the kidnapped rifle, which lay safe and sound some 10 metres away. Pat commented that at least the bull had not shot back at us with it! I must comment here though that you should always take off the rifle's sling before commencing such a hunt. Our intense search for the whole of the next day was in vain and, although I promised the locals a fantastic reward, my record trophy remains only a memory.

The spread of my best buffalo was 45 inches. I bagged it early one morning when I went out on my own. It was still rather dark and the bull was half-facing me. The rifle's foresight was hardly visible but he collapsed under the impact of the 500-grain, solid .458 bullet. After penetrating the four-inch curl of the left horn as if it were a rubber tyre, the bullet then went through the shoulder blade, into the vitals and broke the massive hipbone before lodging under the skin on the opposite side.

I shot my last buffalo in Kenya a few days before my sixtieth birthday when I assisted a friend and former Mweka student with buffalo control at Lake Naivasha. Guided by a game scout, I saw the almost

*Returning from a successful hunt*

hairless, mud-covered, grey colossus in a tiny opening in the papyrus after we had followed a narrow trail over soft, boggy ground. Although its spread measured just over 43 inches, the bosses were enormous. It was also a real monster in body size and, perhaps, it was my best buffalo. Owing to the hunting ban I could not export the head.

It is worth mentioning that the rifle lent to me for that occasion was surely the most distinguished weapon I ever used. It was a custom-made .458 Winchester Magnum, by Holland & Holland, and ordered by President Jomo Kenyatta for the State visit of Yugoslavia's Marshal Tito.

Some years earlier I missed the only chance I ever had to bag a really outstanding bull, a world class buffalo. I was near Lake Manyara where record specimens of *Syncerus caffer* grow. It was late in the evening with the light fading fast. I had my .458 loaded with solids resting firmly against a tree, the open sights of the rifle on the root of a buffalo's tail about 60 metres away, when the buffalo simply walked away from me. On both sides of the body the horns stretched out so wide that it could have been the trophy of my life had the bull only turned just a little sideways. I did not want to bag him with a Texas heart-shot. Almost instantly the acacia-thorns closed behind him and we never saw him again.

The young Sheik, Mohammed Busaidy, a grandson of the Sultan of Zanzibar, from Arabian aristocracy par excellence and my best student at Mweka, was standing behind me and he silently shrugged his shoulders. Later he became a game warden in Kenya and drowned sometime later in the Indian Ocean when he tried to rescue his niece. "Whom the Gods love ..."

Three of us from the College, Brian, Gil and I, attended the funeral in Mombasa in black mourning clothes. The funeral procession was all in white and the corpse in a bundle of white sheets. No women were present. Even his mother, whom I knew well, was absent. There was an unusual, unreal and I would say nearly cheerful atmosphere. Busaidy had been a really good friend of mine and I must have looked sad for his brother stepped forward: "Why do you mourn? It is Allah's will. Allah has called him home."

I still own the two trophies I collected when he was the newly appointed game warden of Voi – a lesser kudu and a really old Oryx with worn horns. In addition, he gave me a whip cut from the skin of a rhino he had shot on control.

## Chapter Three

# Big Tuskers

In the 1920s, an extremely rich, American sportsman told his white hunter, Bror Blixen, who was the husband of the authoress, Tanja Blixen, after he had had an unsuccessful 10-week search for a big elephant, "You can be sure Bror, that I will come back. It's the first time in my life that I pursued something I could not buy. These two and a half months were the best way of passing my time that I've ever had."

Big ivory has always been considered the number one of Africa's big game trophies and the hundred pounder is the measure of all things, its bagging mostly accompanied by jealousy and gossip. Even more than a hundred years ago, Hans Schomburgk, in my opinion the greatest German hunter of African big game, complained how the jealous officials in the then German Dar-es-Salaam screamed blue murder whenever a hunter arrived at the coast with a big pair of tusks.

A concomitant phenomenon, supported by the superstition of the local Maasai, led to the uncovering of a spectacular poaching scandal. The trophy hall of the CAWM claims as one of its top exhibits, the beautifully matched pair of 140 pounds aside tusks confiscated by the Government and generously handed over to Mweka Game School for display. It is ivory with a past.

The bull was shot somewhere in south Maasailand by a game scout on control when a young Englishman, just arrived as district officer from England and responsible for ivory, got himself involved in a disastrous deal with the game scout. The Englishman acquired an elephant licence and, on a weekend trip assisted by the game scout, shot a 30-pounder which, in those days, was a piece of cake.

The tusks were delivered by the scout as a crop-raider killed by himself while the Englishman returned on Sunday night with the sensational 140 pound tusks, the supposed result of his first elephant hunt.

Due to many probing questions and his bad conscience he could not find any peace of mind and, finally, fearing somebody might find the carcass of the 30-pounder, which was much too small for those huge tusks, he returned to the scene of the crime. Having served in the Army as an engineer, he had no problem in blowing up the head of the carcass with a charge of dynamite. But the explosion, which was something completely new and mysterious to them, was heard by some Maasai. Fearing some spell had been placed on their cattle, they immediately went to the authorities in Arusha to report the mystery. In due course, events developed as could have been expected. Regarding ivory fiddles, the authorities would stand no nonsense. The district officer was found guilty, got the sack and was repatriated dishonourably after a lengthy term of imprisonment.

In those days, the game department helplessly tolerated the practice of certain families who bought their annual allocation of two elephant licences, costing 600 E.A. shillings each, for every grown-up member of the clan, including the senile granny in the armchair. Meanwhile they had 'a gun in the bush', meaning an armed African who, with time and patience, lay in wait at waterholes for big tuskers to come and drink. When the whole family, including old granny, finally set out for a weekend safari, the much coveted bull elephant would fall according to plan on Sunday morning, although having been dead for some time. But how was it that these happenings were never stopped? According to Oscar Charlton, game warden of Tanga, the game scouts received far too small a salary to stay honest when tempted.

In one spectacular case the fraud was discovered. Game Warden Eric Balson succeeded in proving that a pair of tusks brought by the licence holder, an African police officer, to the boma at Iringa, was actually killed by a poacher in the Ruaha National Park in 1971. With a combined weight of 381 pounds (192 and 189 pound respectively), they were the second heaviest pair of tusks on record.

The big elephants arrived in western Tanzania mainly at the beginning of the rains in October. Nobody knew where they came from

*My best tusks weighing 112 lbs and 103 lbs from Maasailand*

nor where they disappeared to in the endless brachystegia woodland which, in Kiswaheli, is called *miombo*. In the thousands of square kilometres of wilderness and deserted tsetse bush, no light at night or pillar of smoke in daytime betrayed human settlement. It was a timeless, forgotten land in which gigantic animals that weighed up to six tons were lost like specks of dust.

*Thousands of square miles of tsetse bush and empty wilderness*

At night, when the horizon was illuminated by the sheet lightning of distant thunderstorms and huge, almost hand-sized moths bounced against the paraffin lamps, we knew the dry season would not last much longer. Towards the end, the sultry heat was almost intolerable and, bathed in sweat, I would listen to the first thunder claps which announced the arrival of the rainy season.

What a relief! The refreshing drumming of water onto tents and roofs. When the downpour ceased, an indescribable scent of steaming soil, wet ash and opening flowers filled the air. This was the time to set out for the remote localities where the ripening fruit of the Borassus palm would attract elephants from far and wide. This was the chance to go and test your wits against the mightiest and most intelligent game animals on earth, hoping to find that legendary tusker that native honey hunters told fantastic stories about around the campfires at night – a fascinating challenge par excellence.

Being in top physical condition, equipped only with the lightest necessities and free of the tyranny of possessions, I could walk continuously for more than 20 miles a day, through thick and thin, trusting in my reliable Mauser rifle as well as my small team of seasoned Africans, although I sometimes had to smile at their superstitions regarding hunting dangerous game. But I too had experiences I could not comprehend, occurrences I just could not explain, events absolutely beyond my comprehension.

*My biggest tusker (very old bull) before the shot*

On 15 October 1958, near Massanza, the little village near Lake Tanganyika where the bloody depredations of a notorious man-eating lion had taken place, I had been following the spoor of three elephants for hours with my two trackers, Nasoro Mmeta and Bambala, but we just could not catch up with them. It was terribly hot and, at about 3 o'clock in the afternoon when we lost the spoor, I gave up, completely exhausted and parched.

Nasoro, a Mnyamwezi, who had an incredible sense of direction, led us slowly back to camp. Heaven knows how far away it was but, after a short while, he stopped dead. At the end of a small grassy plain there stood the three bulls under a tall tree. Two were fair-sized animals but one towered over his companions. He was a real giant whose tusks almost touched the ground. I guessed that they would weigh at least 120 pounds aside and I rejoiced, meanwhile forgetting that the position in which the bull stood always made the tusks look bigger.

The wind was perfect and, during these hottest hours of the day, I was certain they would rest there for a good while, quiet and with no movement except the occasional flapping of the huge, sail-like ears which are cooling mechanisms. But, while I was still whispering to Nasoro, all of a sudden and without the slightest indication of any concern, the old bull walked determinedly away. His two askaris followed rather reluctantly.

Without hesitation and leaving my trackers behind, I started to

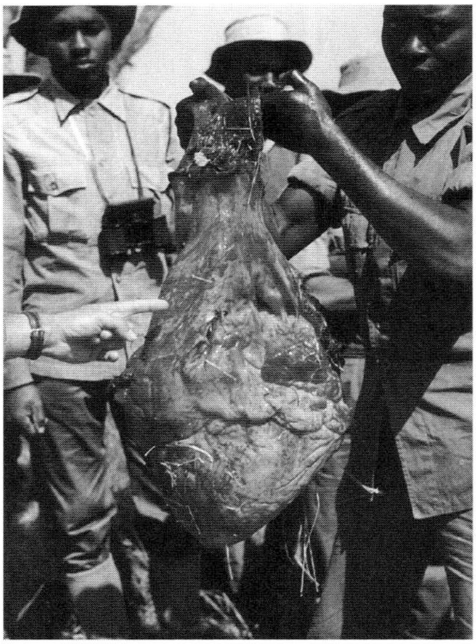

*An elephant's heart*

*My first hundred pounder, 1958 (with author's daughter, Katharina)*

run on a parallel course about 80 metres from the fast-walking beasts whose course took them through a dense stand of trees. Amazingly I was not tired any more. In my right hand, I carried my rifle, a .404 by Alex Henry of Edinburgh and, in my left, the ashbag.

After some 150 metres I passed the big bull and turned towards him. I stopped behind a tree on which to rest the rifle as I was too exhausted to risk an offhand shot. And there they came. In a few seconds the big one would pass me broadside on at an easy range. I felt suddenly triumphant. Now at last I have got him I thought. Nothing could go wrong now but, at that moment, he turned away from me without the slightest hesitation in his gait or any sign of disquiet or suspicion. With no time to think, I fired a quartering shot into the middle of his ribs, the last and only chance left. It was a shot I had never taken before and I prayed my solid bullet would reach the vitals. The result was a lightning turn, a thundering flight and crashing trees which hid the bull in a whirling cloud of dust. I had no chance for a second shot.

I was finished, unable to think and in absolute despair. All those hard, bitter hours and days on the elephants' trail and now, in a few seconds, everything was ruined. I knew that I would never see this mighty bull again!

*Elephant control with Bambala and Nasoro (right)*

But then the two trackers came running to draw me forward with them. I could hardly believe my eyes, there, hardly 200 metres away, stood the two askaris next to the giant that was swaying on his feet. I gave him two finishing bullets into the heart as a *coup de grâce* and he collapsed with a loud thud. Only when I sent Nasoro upwind did the two askaris, rather hesitatingly, leave their dead patriarch.

I just could not stop staring at the splendid tusks, which weighed 102 and 94 pounds, while Nasoro danced around the dead beast. But I had to step aside as I was suddenly so sick from exhaustion and excitement that I had to vomit. "That is the ghost of the elephant taking its revenge," I heard Nasoro whisper to Bambala.

Even today, I cannot understand why the old bull, against all norms, suddenly ended his siesta during the heat of the day without having got our wind. What was also a mystery was that, after I had cut off his escape route and hardly a second before I could aim for his heart, he turned instantly away when he could neither have scented nor seen me. Was it a sixth-sense that allowed him to foresee the danger, or perhaps some vibration emanating from me which warned him of his mortal enemy? Perhaps it is a good thing that in nature there are still occurrences beyond our comprehension.

Much later I gave a lecture to hunters in South Tyrol and showed

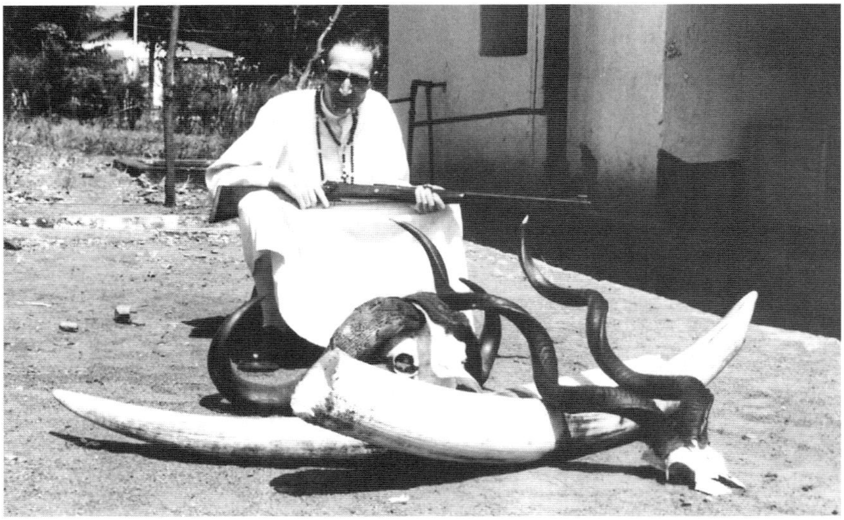

*Father Francis Tryers with some of the author's trophies*

the slide with me posing in front of that elephant. An old hunter who had served under Mussolini in Ethiopia called out, "Ye, weren't you still a youngster?"

Some time before this lucky hunt I was in charge of a team spraying along the coastal shrubs of Lake Tanganyika. After spending the whole week on the lake supervising my 20 labourers, I returned on Saturday around noon, had a hasty lunch and proceeded in my Land Rover some 80 miles into the wilds, to the northeast of Kigoma, to hunt elephants on licence. We were allowed two per year for a licence fee of 600 E.A. shillings each.

I had only Sunday morning to hunt as, in the evening, I had to return to work on the lake the next day. But I was soon to discover that this arrangement was in total disagreement with my very pious wife who strongly resented me missing Holy Mass on Sundays to chase after elephants.

As it happened, I had just returned one Sunday evening from an uneventful outing when we had a visit from our local priest, the Rev. Father Francis Tryers from the White Father's Mission at Ujiji who, unbeknown to my wife, was also a keen hunter. Thinking this to be her chance, she immediately asked him whether it was compatible with the rules of the church to neglect the compulsory attendance of Sunday's Mass in order to chase elephants. The clergyman's answer must have come as a shock to her for it was quite different from what she had hoped for. "Well, Mrs Hecker," he replied with the most solemn face, "if your husband is pursuing a hundred pounder then, I think, the Lord wouldn't mind."

Father Tryers, who baptized my second daughter at Ujiji, became a dear friend of the family and, when on home leave in later years, often visited us in Germany. Poor Francis, instead of finding his last resting place in his beloved Buha, died miserably of stomach cancer in London. During his last months he lived almost entirely on cigarettes and tea.

*An African elephant – ever captivating*

## Chapter Four

# Elephant Hunting
## Past and Present

At the beginning of colonial rule, in about 1890, African elephant hunters were legally entitled to pursue the dangerous beasts with muzzle-loaders. In 1898, Senoussi, who was hunting on behalf of the infamous slave trader, Shundi, bagged the all time world record on the slopes of Mount Kilimanjaro, an elephant with tusks that weighed 226 and 214 pounds aside, which can be seen in the British National History Museum in London.

There were a number of black, professional ivory hunters called *Fundis*, *Makuas* or *Malumbas*. Admired as rich men, they were also recognized as brave and fearless hunters. Some 130 years ago, the people of Mahenge, in Tanzania, changed their name to Mangula, which was the name of the bold *fundi* who finally succeeded in killing a ferocious, bull elephant that had killed several tribesmen. It was generally believed that these brave hunters must be in possession of a powerful charm obtained from a top class witch-doctor.

Although most *fundis* believed that death in the bush was the will of God, after killing about 15 tuskers they often willingly left their risky profession to younger men and henceforth used their fame to produce fetishes and charms which would provide its owner with courage and self-confidence.

The well-known physician, Albert Schweitzer from Lambarene, in West Africa, wrote in 1920 that the belief prevailed among professional elephant hunters that each bagging of an elephant, necessitated a fetish and the most powerful fetish was part of the skull of a human specifically killed for the preparation of the fetish. That meant that, to achieve the necessary fetish, an elephant hunter would have to become a murderer.

In the old days, the rate of casualties was considered to be one

*Gobore hunter in western Tanzania (Buha)*

dead hunter to about every 50 elephants killed, a high number compared with the one or two game scouts who lost their lives annually around 1960 when shooting some 3 000 elephants on control. Of course, they were issued with modern .404 rifles and were given appropriate training while the old *fundis* had to rely on crude muzzle-loaders or poisoned arrows.

I don't know whether nowadays, after civil wars and corruption have flooded Africa with AK47s, elephants are still hunted with old muzzle-loaders surviving from the Arab era. We found that some of the elephants I shot in western Tanzania had old projectiles of different shapes embedded in their flesh or skulls and heaven knows how many elephant bulls carried these crude pieces of iron around with them, perhaps for years.

Early muzzle-loading hunters carried mostly muskets, the stock, if broken, being held together by wire, thin metal sheets or leather and these chaps often showed injuries, like missing front teeth or a crippled hand, caused by an overload of black powder. During the Maji-Maji uprising in January 1907, the former elephant hunter and much dreaded rebel leader, Abdalla Mapanda, was killed in an ambush. The Germans displayed his right hand on a spear blade at Liwale market as proof of the death of the legendary hero. The thumb was missing and it was generally known that it was lost when his overcharged muzzle-loader burst.

These hunters were, of course, top guides and trackers found among subsistence hunters and gatherers, who were usually considered by their 'civilized' black brethren to be 'washensi', wild and uneducated men from the bush. Those in Tanzania were predominantly from the Wandorobo (comparable to the Bushmen from the Kalahari or the Pygmies from the Congo in tracking and hunting ability), and the Wakamba and Waliangulu were from Kenya. Some excellent trackers were also found among the pastoral tribes, like the Maasai or Wangoni, who are descendants of the South African Zulu.

Maasai children practised the tracking down of centipedes, scorpions and beetles as a way of passing the time. Growing up, they had to tend goats and sheep and woe betide them when an animal was missing in the evening. Understandably, at an early age, they learned to follow the tiny spoor of kids or lambs and they grew up, quite naturally, with the art of tracking.

Many white hunters had Maasai or Ndorobo trackers on their permanent staff. Pat Hemingway once remarked that, to be fair, the names of the trackers should be placed before the owner of the trophy in Rowland Ward's *Records of Big Game*. In most cases they would not have been taken without their bushcraft. I quite often felt inferior when faced with the art of hunting displayed by these half-naked, primitive people, especially when hunting bongo in Congo-Brazzaville. I was disappointed when later I heard of the fate of my top tracker, Makanya, a pygmy, who was banished from his clan and just disappeared. Apparently, while living in a lumber camp he had, while drunk, made use of a mechanical chain-saw to amputate the arm of his wife – technical progress in the primeval forest!

Another outstanding tracker I remember is Mabondo from Nyaviumbu, near Kibondo, who followed the tracks of a crop-raiding bull elephant so instinctively and fast that I was hardly able to

*On elephant control with the shamba owners*

keep pace. Mabondo had no reputation as a tracker and was up to then unknown to me but, being the owner of the devastated fields, he guided me without being asked and as a matter of course.

That suited me very well as I had no driver, game scout or gun bearer with me. After about two hours we came up to the solitary bull but, due to the high grass after the heavy rainy season, I had to shoot from the top of a rather pointed termite mound, balancing without having a firm stand and aiming for the heart at about 30 metres. The recoil of the .458 sent me over backwards down the side of the mound, fortunately, right into the arms of the quick-witted Mabondo.

Soon the noise of the fleeing beast ceased without the sound of it collapsing and, with mixed feelings, we had to follow the wounded animal. There was very little blood on the ground but Mabondo ran on the tracks so fast that I could hardly follow, especially as I had to peer sideways as well as in front.

Suddenly I saw the elephant's outline behind the thick foliage while Mabondo was five or six metres in front of me. I managed to stop him just in time with a low call as he would have walked right underneath the trunk which was rolled up ready to strike. Immediately the bull charged from its cover and I dropped it with a brain shot. It was an old, single tusker of enormous body size. Its

*An old bull in the ideal position for a side on brain shot*

tusk was very thick and weighed 60 pounds while the other was a broken and hollow piece weighing 28 pounds. Like all ivory from control hunting, the tusks were the property of the Government.

I would like to now say a few words about the oft-mentioned elephant control. After World War I, the pachyderms in southern and eastern Tanzania increased to such an extent that, in certain areas, the agricultural damage reached alarming proportions. In 1923, a first counter-measure failed when a few European hunters were offered free licences to each shoot 25 elephants with one tusk of each being handed to the Government. But without stricter regulations these sportsmen mainly pursued big tuskers, often in areas far from the endangered fields. In about 1928, the so-called cultivation protectors, who were later called game wardens, were employed in one or two heavily raided provinces. On their staff were 10 to 15 African game scouts, trained as elephant hunters, who were supposed to shoot the culprits.

With the growing numbers of settlements, the situation escalated in such a way that, around 1965, about 3 000 elephants had to be shot annually for crop protection. To begin with, the scouts used .303 calibre British service rifles but were later issued with Martini-

*As close as possible - and then another 10 metres closer*
*(author on an elephant hunt in Tanzania)*

*Elephant control*

Henry, single-shot .577/.450 falling-block rifles and, from 1929 onwards, these were replaced by magazine Vickers .404s.

Certain scouts shot several hundred crop raiders during their period of service. Their skill at being able to approach to very close range was often more important than accuracy in aiming, especially as quite a few hunters believed that the muzzle-flash was deadlier than the bullet itself. An average of three rounds per kill was considered satisfactory. In one year, Head Game Scout, Mbeya Sulemani from Liwale, shot 30 crop-raiders with 29 rounds, one of them exiting to kill a second elephant. However, during a later shooting exercise, it became obvious that Mbeya did not need to use the open sights of his rifle. He stalked so close to his quarry that he would probably have hit the mark even with his eyes shut.

At CAWM, I once had to train Frederic Petro who, from his early childhood, accompanied his father, a famous elephant hunting game scout from Ubena. But I almost despaired on the range when Frederic could hardly hit the target at 30 metres with a .22 and I was more than sceptical when, before the first control safari, I issued him with a .458. I let Frederic go only under the supervision of an experienced elephant scout and then, on the third day, Frederic shot five elephants within a few minutes!

The ivory from control hunting produced a considerable income

*Frederic Petro (left) shot 5 elephants in 3 minutes on elephant control*

for the Government. At the end of the 1960s, however, the game department no longer received an allocation of money to buy ammunition and, as a result, the necessary and very lucrative crop protection came to an end. Only the control safaris of the CAWM continued due to foreign aid which was just a drop in the ocean. The elephant problem was soon to be solved, however, by large scale ivory poaching in the 1970s. In 1980, when I hunted with my friend, Kurt, in the Kingupira area of the Selous, we picked up more than 20 tusks of beasts that had been wounded during the rainy season from outboard motor boats on the Ruaha and Rufiji rivers.

I shot my first elephant (with ivory of 63 and 62 pounds aside), in 1956, on licence, near the Great Ruaha river without a backing rifle as my two trackers disappeared when I began the final stalk. Quite early, when working for the Tsetse Department, I started helping out with control work as the game warden at Tabora only managed to visit his scouts once or twice a year. Most of them were top hunters, some of whom still used muzzle-loaders.

The muzzle-loading hunters made a habit of approaching their quarry up to ranges of about 10 metres as, further than that, the inaccuracy of their antiquated guns became a factor. Another reason behind their accuracy was the high price of black powder and lead. Each miss meant a severe loss as they could not recover

*Ivory from a control hunt (Alexander Frumbe on the left)*

the bullet from the body of the shot animal. Whenever they were found in skulls or when cutting up meat, the old projectiles quickly vanished to be reactivated again, especially as the hunters were now convinced of their proven efficiency .

When training our students at CAWM we often went unarmed to Kenya's Tsavo National Park, which was just across the border, to practice the stalking of elephants, basing our teaching on the old adage 'get as close as you can and then get 10 metres closer'. We also wanted to get the students used to being close to elephants and to teach them the proper assessment of sex and age.

When on control it was predominantly the young bulls and females without calves that were eliminated with heart shots. During our control training every student, assisted by an instructor or experienced game scout, was supposed to shoot at least one buffalo and two elephants. These operations mainly took place in the Kilombero valley, the Umba plains near Tanga or the mist forests of Mount Meru. While we fortunately never had an accident, occasionally some amusing incidents took place.

I led Alexander Frumbe towards a single bull standing in an open grassy plain, some 30 or 40 metres from a solitary tree, against which the young Cameroonian could rest his rifle. I stayed a short way behind and waited for him to make the easy shot. Frumbe

*Stalking elephants (unarmed) with future game wardens*

*Coup de grâce. Notice the recoil of the .458*

aimed for an eternity until the elephant became restless and turned to walk away. As it had to be shot for control purposes, I felled the beast with a brain-shot and called out ironically, "Congratulations, good shot!" At this Frumbe turned around and answered, "Oh, thank you very much, Sir!" Whether he meant my shot or my congratulations I do not know and his comrades, watching from a far away termite mound, never found out the real story.

After every safari there was a question time in the classroom and events were discussed, analysed and criticized. During one, student Mosha, a brilliant, know-all schoolboy from Tanga, said, "Sir, you have called me a bloody fool!"

It was a few moments before I remembered, "Oh yeah, very sorry, I apologize!"

So what had happened? The same situation occurred as with Alexander Frumbe, the only difference being that I did not shoot. It was a middle-aged bull, standing broadside on, in open brachystegia woodland, at 20 metres range. An ideal situation for an easy heart shot.

Mosha was behind a tree with a good rifle rest. I stood behind, not hurrying him but giving him time, maybe too much time, which might have made him nervous. I finally whispered, "Shoot." Then again, "Shoot." Still no action and, eventually, the elephant became

*Results of a control hunt in the Kilombero Valley with the CAWM Gill Child in the centre (with a light shirt) and the author is next to him*

fidgety so I said louder, "Shoot, you bloody fool!" The laughter in the classroom would not end when I told them the story and I think that Mosha regretted the complaint.

Incidentally, again and again the students declared that the recoil of the .458 was horrible when target shooting on the range but hardly noticeable while shooting at game.

After a hectic hunt, which ended with me having to stop a charging elephant cow which fell almost at our feet, the two young Kenyans who were with me remarked, rather trustingly, that I surely must have a very strong heart and nerves of steel. Whereupon I would have liked to answer, "My God, if you only knew ...!" During practical hunting, the difference between the schoolboys just arrived from secondary school and candidates sent by the game departments, was striking. Apart from the latter having difficulties with their English – a precondition to join CAWM – in the bush they were definitely superior, in the same way that the schoolboys were better in our classes.

Sometimes we noticed a tendency among some academically top students to consider manual labour to be beneath them, like mending a puncture, erecting a tent or cutting up game, an attitude the European instructors always tried to influence by their partici-

*Elephant shot on control*

pation in such jobs. Let me conclude this subject with a little story about the already mentioned Dr Albert Schweitzer, taken from John Gunther's, *Inside Africa*.

> "Once, when most of his helpers were ill, Schweitzer had to drag some heavy beams under cover before an outburst of tropical rain. This was tedious physical labour. The doctor noticed a Negro in a white suit sitting near a patient whom he had come to visit. Schweitzer called out, "Hello friend! Won't you lend us a hand?" The Negro replied, "I don't drag wood about. I am an intellectual". Schweitzer replied, "How lucky you are. I tried to be an intellectual, too, but didn't succeed."

To return to the issue of elephant control. I have often been asked why the hunting of some of these control elephants was not sold to overseas sport hunters. Well, 40 years ago, nobody in the game department of Tanzania imagined that sportsmen from overseas would spend money to shoot small bulls or female elephants, especially as the income from such hunts would never have covered the expenses. Outsiders often believe that the shooting of cull elephants is an easy affair, comparatively cheap and not as

*Elephant shot on control*

dangerous and exhausting as the search for a big tusker. They misjudged the real situation with its logistical and organizational problems, circumstances which very often made control hunting or crop protection very hard jobs.

The necessary shooting had to be done when the elephants caused the damage to the crops and that was in the rainy season or, shortly thereafter, in grass of at least two metres. Many roads and tracks were impassable then due to heavy downpours and certain valleys were difficult to negotiate, especially those with soggy, black cotton soil. Often you could reach the operational areas only with porters, their tents and food having to be carried as well.

The normal tourist-hunter could hardly imagine what happened in the period of the 'long rains'. Sometimes at night I lay on my camp bed, torrential rain roaring down, only to wake up at daybreak to the drumming choir of thousands of frogs and to watch, rather helplessly through the mosquito net, as water flowed slowly through the tent, fortunately not reaching my clothing and guns which I placed on my safari chairs. And that despite the drainage ditches we dug around the tents.

The humidity was so 'thick' that, when the guns were taken out of their canvas covers, they immediately got steamed up and I was glad that we only used magazine rifles with the indestructible Mauser 98 action and open sights. Even when it was not raining in the morning, soon after leaving the camp we got sopping wet, right up to our necks, from the cold dew on the grass. Often the gun bearers had to hold the rifles above their heads to keep them dry.

With the rising sun, the tsetse flies became active and irritating. When walking in single file, the person behind you carried a branch as a fly-whisk to chase away the hungry blood-suckers which attacked necks and shoulders as a matter of preference, their bites being quite painful even through our thin khaki shirts.

We mostly camped near villages known for being raided. Often the nightly visitors gave themselves away by their foraging noises in the maize or millet fields and banana plantations. We would start tracking at daybreak. With luck we would soon catch up with bulls that were mostly small but, more often than not, it would take a couple of hours by which time the wind was tricky and, if they got our wind, we would not catch up with them at all.

Sometimes local guides, who were well acquainted with the locality, would lead us (without following the raiders' tracks), directly to a certain spot where they expected the elephants to spend the day, mainly in small basins or valleys at the foot of a hill. As if aware of impending danger after their nightly depredations, the elephants would occasionally retreat into almost impenetrable thickets. In one case, I remember it was a swamp with horribly high *matete* grass. After a difficult follow-up, I was lucky to meet the leading bull of a small bachelor group face to face at short range. Hit in the brain, his hindquarters gave way, followed by the forepart of the body and he toppled over on his side. To avoid the remaining four or five beasts who were milling around unseen, my tracker and I quickly climbed the sloping hind leg onto the top of the hopefully dead elephant, from where I succeeded in shooting two more bulls with heart-shots.

If there were no nightly alarms, in the morning we listened for drum beats from hamlets in the vicinity or waited for reports brought in by runners. When nothing happened for a day or two, we were not unhappy to rest from the sometimes very strenuous hunts, especially when a wounded beast had to be followed, which occurred mainly from taking shots at too long a range. Although I continually preached that the maximum shooting range was 20 metres and to take heart-shots instead of brain-shots (the brain-shot offering too small a target), the new boys did not fancy being so close to an elephant.

We also tried to shoot only cows that were not with calves. Even today, after so many years, I am haunted by the pitiful sight of an orphaned calf. These I killed with a quick shot to spare the poor creatures the painful agony of mostly unsuccessful hand-rearing.

As it would have been useless to ask the reasons for the tragedy, I tried to comfort myself with the saying, 'One can't make an omelette without breaking eggs'. But during crop protection we mostly had to deal with males, mainly young 'hooligans' circling like satellites, at a distance of up to 20 kilometres, around the breeding herds. The old and experienced cows were usually too wise to move too close to human habitation.

When it became obvious that increased culling of bulls had a negative influence on the sex ratio and the annual increment of the population became alarmingly small, the culling of females seemed to be inevitable. The best time for this undertaking was when the rains started. This filled the waterholes and brought on the first flush of green grass and foliage, thus triggering the elephant herds to move away from the dry season concentration areas.

Tracking became much easier than it was during the drought months with its hard ground. We tried to tackle the smaller herds and to shoot as many suitable females as possible. But now we more often met with more critical situations than when hunting bulls. Even without small calves at their heels, the cows were always more aggressive than the opposite sex. The human losses during elephant control were two to three game scouts per annum, which were mostly caused by cows, especially in thick *machaka*, as the dense, evergreen clumps of bush in the forest were called. On one occasion I was very lucky. I was stalking ahead of my tracker when I saw what at first sight I thought was a python above my head but which was, in reality, an elephant's trunk descending from a low treetop as if to grasp my hat. Only at the shortest distance did I observe the outline of the cow and, luckily for me, she behaved peacefully.

Owing to the necessity of reducing numbers, we tried to cull as many from a herd as possible and, to achieve this, the herd's matriarch – provided she didn't have a small calf – had to be felled first with a brain-shot. The remainder of the herd was then confused by not having a leader to follow and stood still or milled around, offering the chance for body shots. If the matriarch was heart-shot, she would run for 50 to 70 metres before collapsing when, of course, she was followed in full flight by the others in the herd.

The carcasses were left for consumption by the meat-hungry populations as a form of compensation for the damage to their fields. It was amazing how fast the news of a kill spread as often, only a few hours after the shooting, a long row of natives following each other in single file would turn up. It always made me wonder how they knew where the kill was and I could only presume that they must have used the sight of high circling vultures to guide them. The men all carried axes, pangas and knives while the woman came with children on their backs and calabashes filled with water

*An elephant control 'by-product'*

balanced on their heads.

As soon as the tusks were cut out and the ears removed for use as leather, the carcass was free for butchering. At night numerous campfires flared up around the 'battlefield'. The meat was stripped from the bones and smoked over fires till dry before being packed into long bundles, tied with bark string, to be carried home on the heads of the women.

If the elephant carcasses could not be utilized due to the long distance from habitation, the meat was not left unused or wasted. For two to three weeks the carcasses offered food to all the predators, from lions to jackals, as well as vultures and marabou storks, while the normal prey species in the vicinity were left unmolested. During crop protection, private licence hunting for elephant, rhino or leopard was prohibited. The bagging of other game, if it did not interfere with our control work, was however tolerated. Even today, my mouth waters when I remember that record Maasai bushbuck standing almost provocatively before me in the mist forest of

Mount Meru. I could not take it because the buffalo tracks we were following were too fresh, their droppings still warm and any moment we expected to make contact. Later I devoted several weekend hunts to find that huge bushbuck but I never saw it again.

On the way back from the Malagarasi, while walking in front of my porters, there stood a pitch black sable bull in a small, open clearing hardly a hundred metres away, its enormous horns curving almost to its hindquarters. I judged them to be over 45 inches long, while my best sable at that time measured 41 inches. The bull was accompanied by three or four cows which, in contrast to the male, were a beautiful, reddish brown colour. Before I could get hold of my 9.3x62 Mauser, such a sudden torrential rain poured down that I could hardly see the sights of my rifle or the fleeing game and when, after half an hour, the cloudburst stopped, all the tracks had been washed away.

My encounter with a lone buffalo bull, which had the most massive boss I had ever seen ended similarly. The intervention of that heavy rainstorm almost certainly saved the life of that bull. Despite frantic searching for hours after the rain stopped, it was as if the bull had vanished into thin air.

*Unusual white giraffe*

## Chapter Five

# Black Magic
## Superstition and Hunting

Quite early in our time in Africa, my wife and I were confronted by the deeply-rooted superstitions of the Africans. A relative of our house servant was arrested and the whole family got into a panic. The lad, a 20-year-old Catholic, had visited his aunt who had the reputation of being a witch. She lived in the Highlands of Iringa and, according to traditional hospitality, she served him a bowl of soup. After he had eaten it, the old woman admitted she had poisoned the soup on account of some quarrel in the remote past and said he would, in due course, die.

Horror-stricken, the youngster immediately ran downhill through the game-filled Uchungwe Mountains to the Ifakara mission in the Kilombero Valley. Almost paralysed with fear he reported his misfortune to the Swiss Capuchin monks. They kept him there for the night after having administered an 'absolutely effective remedy' in the form of some Aspirin pills and released the boy 'as completely cured' the next morning.

But his superstitious dread of the sinister powers of darkness was stronger than his Christian belief. He hurried straight back to Uhehe, stormed into his aunt's hut and screamed, "I will not die alone." And he beheaded the old crone with one stroke of his panga. Accused of manslaughter and not murder, when he would have been hanged, he was imprisoned for some years as, in those days, the British judges showed a remarkable understanding and sympathy for defendants suffering from such sinister obsessions.

The origins of witchcraft lie perhaps in the search by primitive people for security and protection from the elementary forces of nature like lightning, flood, drought, fire, locusts and man-eating lions that, according to their belief, are triggered by evil spirits. Moreover, they seek to maintain a close alliance with their ancestors through their witchdoctors who act as mediums, which is the reason why sorcerers of both sexes play important roles in many parts of Africa even today. When called for, they often arrive in intimidating robes covered with gruesome fetishes like monkey tails, snake skins, skulls of vultures and the teeth of carnivores but their most important and indispensable piece of equipment is a bag containing small vertebrae of ritually killed mammals. Throwing the bones is like playing at dice, the magician can tell the future from their position on the ground or determine the identity of a searched for culprit.

To be fair, it has to be said that besides these sinister individuals there are today in Africa many more traditional healers, known as herbalists, who operate quite successfully with their inherited knowledge of preparing medicines out of 119 known species of flora. In 1981, I wrote in an article about a man-eater in the magazine, *Wild und Hund*, in which I said: "Africa, still so dark and unfathomable despite 100 years of missionary work, modern technologies and economic aid. Or is this only the opinion of Europeans obsessed by the delusion of progress and not having lived long enough out there to understand how superficial their knowledge of the country is, how little they know about its people and their mentality."

Whilst I was writing these lines for this book in August 2002, the British Sunday Telegraph reported from Zimbabwe that, by the raping of hundreds of women and girls, the village to which they belonged was being punished by President Mugabe's party for poor voting results in the elections.

In the superstitious imagination of many Africans sex plays a dominant role, for example the rule of strict abstinence during wars and before hunting dangerous game. During the Maji-Maji uprising of 1905 to 1907, when the German askaris shot the rebels by the dozen, the infuriated witchdoctors explained that the failure of their medicine, which was supposed to turn the askaris' bullets into water, was due to the failure to adhere to sexual abstinence. According to the famous big game hunter, Jim Sutherland, the violation of this rule automatically triggers the fatal attack of elephants or buffaloes and it has spread from West to East Africa. Before following up a wounded buffalo in high grass, the German army officer, Hans Paasche, asked his tracker whether he was afraid,

*Nasoro with two ancestor huts, complete with offerings of flour for the road*

to which the African replied, "Why should we be? Before the hunt none of us had the chance to visit a prostitute."

Due to this superstition I once lost a big elephant in eastern Tanzania during the rainy season in 1959. I had set out early with my Mnyawezi tracker, Nasoro Mmeta. While bringing up the rear, my porter, Bambala, noticed that some three metres to my left lay a coiled up black mamba with its slender head raised, watching me. The name derives from the black colour of the inside of its mouth. I just walked quietly on and then showed the two Africans, from a safe distance, where I had seen the mamba which we, of course, left undisturbed. "It is a bad omen," was their only comment, which amused me.

Some time later, we stopped dead when a big leopard slowly crossed a small, open clearing in front of us. Because of the wet grass its tail was up and arched to keep it dry. Entranced by the unusual encounter, I was nevertheless a bit annoyed with Nasoro's remark, uttered with a wrinkled up face, "This again is a very bad sign!"

At last we came up with two fresh elephant tracks, one with a diameter of 60 cm, a really outstanding size. I was full of hope as I expected to meet the elephant soon as their droppings were still warm, and juicy food, shade and water was plentiful everywhere.

Around noon we crossed some older tracks and broken down branches with dried up foliage which meant that we had to track very carefully, thus making little progress. Then I noticed that the trackers were following the tracks from the day before, which was confirmed by cold dung. I took Nasoro to task. He looked very embarrassed as we had lost precious time and also because a dark-blue weather front had risen ominously behind bright, white cloud formations and, within minutes, we were engulfed in a cloudburst. I turned my rifle upside down and put the muzzle onto my boot to keep it dry.

When the downpour ceased, we shook ourselves like wet dogs and tried to find the washed out tracks. Unexpectedly, we heard the sound of a tree branch breaking. Testing the wind with a wetted finger as my ashbag was drenched, I checked my Westley Richards .458 and took the lead.

We had to cross a flooded stream with the water up to our knees. I knew it was full of leeches and tied my trousers tight around the ankles to stop the leeches getting inside and sucking my blood. Out of breath, I climbed a low rise that the two trackers had already scaled. They were waving excitedly to me to hurry up. There, about 120 metres away, at the base of a large termite mound, I saw a giant of an elephant. His tusks jutted at least two feet out of the jaw and were as thick as a man's thigh right up to their points.

I desperately looked for a tree to rest my rifle on as an offhand shot at that distance in my exhausted condition would have been irresponsible. The bull already had his trunk up testing the wind. With ears spread he quickly showed us his disappearing hindquarters and I remembered again the comment when we saw the leopard, 'this again is a very bad sign'. I presumed that, because of their superstition, the trackers 'knew' I would not get the bull and had acted in an irresponsible manner behind me which had given us away.

I experienced the consequences of this superstition in a grotesque form in Kigoma where the still sprightly police constable, Petro Kamili, lived as a pensioner. Due to his spotless period of service he had been granted the ownership of a .404 calibre rifle, an amazing fact as, in those days, Africans were very rarely permitted to purchase rifles, although they were permitted to own shotguns.

Petro, whom I knew well and met sometimes after church in Kigoma, shot his two licensed elephants annually and I wondered why he often brought rather meagre-sized ivory to the boma for registration. He always hunted them close to the shores of Lake Tanganyika from where he could smuggle the smoked meat across the lake into the Congo, with these profits compensating well for the low value of the ivory from the elephants he shot.

Once, when I returned from a lengthy safari, the fathers of Kigoma Mission told me that Petro had returned from a hunt foaming with rage and had beaten his wife almost to death. He claimed to have escaped a charging elephant by a hair's breadth which, of course, meant there could be no doubt about it – during his absence his wife must have been unfaithful to him. Any other explanation for the elephant's attack was absolutely out of the question. The wife's family kept quiet because the victim found free treatment at the mission hospital. And I have no doubt that, as the relatives were also steeped in superstition, they too were convinced of the wife's misconduct.

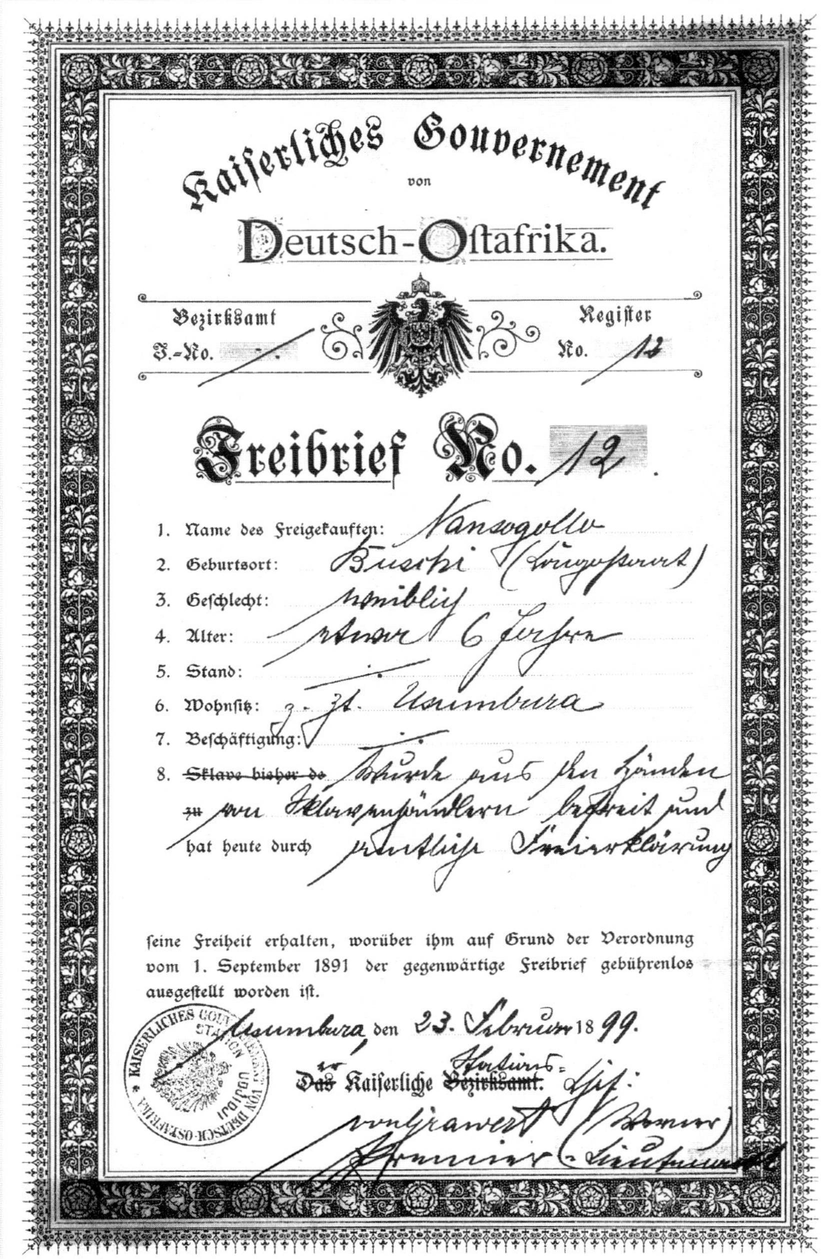
Kaiserliches Gouvernement von Deutsch-Ostafrika.

Bezirksamt J.-No. —

Register No. 12

Freibrief No. 12.

1. Name des Freigekauften: Nansogollo
2. Geburtsort: Busiki ([illegible])
3. Geschlecht: weiblich
4. Alter: etwa 6 Jahre
5. Stand: —
6. Wohnsitz: z. Zt. Usumbura
7. Beschäftigung: —
8. ~~Sklave bisher de~~ wurde aus den Händen ~~zu~~ von Sklavenhändlern befreit und hat heute durch amtliche Freierklärung

seine Freiheit erhalten, worüber ihm auf Grund der Verordnung vom 1. September 1891 der gegenwärtige Freibrief gebührenlos ausgestellt worden ist.

Usumbura, den 23. Februar 1899.

~~Das~~ Der Kaiserliche ~~Bezirksamt~~ Stations-Chef.

von Grawert (Premier-Lieutenant)

KAISERLICHES GOUVERNEMENT VON DEUTSCH-OSTAFRIKA STATION USUMBURA

## Chapter Six

# Missionaries, Slaves and Ivory

I will always remember with gratitude those people who assisted me in the remotest wilderness and offered me hospitality whenever I turned up. These were the missionaries of different orders, like the Capucins, the White Fathers and Consolata Fathers whose stations I got to know as strongholds of civilization and enlightenment in a dark world of superstition and inhumane witchcraft. They were brave men whom I still admire today.

In modern and enlightened times, political scientists and psychologists compete to critically investigate the role of missionaries in the early and post-colonial epochs. In this context I would like to quote the words of Nigel Barley, a noted English ethnologist: "Regarding missionaries, young ethnologists already know more about them before they have even seen one."

Due to my personal friendship with many missionaries, I prefer to comment from my own experience and to quote Murray-Smith, doyen of the white hunters of Kenya, who wrote in his book, *Forty Years Among African Game* (Paul Parey 1964): "My stay at the Lukuledi Mission in Tanzania increased my deepest respects for these selfless and devoted men, sacrificing their lives for the improvement of the spiritual and material existence of the native people of the Interior without any hope of personal reward on earth. When saying 'Goodbye' I asked the father superior when his next leave would be due. His answer: 'When I die, my son!'"

I once presented the White Father from Ushirombo with a nice buffalo trophy and, in return, he gave me a rare document, the *freiheitsbrief* (Freedom letter) of a young African girl named Nansogollo that had been issued free of charge by the Imperial German Government of Deutsch-Ostafrika on 23 February 1899. Over 100 years ago, the freed slave girl had found shelter and protection in

*"...one quarrelsome wife is enough for me!" How strong willed must the Sultan of Oudjila have been with his 27 wives (they did not all fit into the picture!), taken many years ago in Northern Cameroon*

Ushirombo Mission.

To come back to the *freiheitsbrief*, the beautifully printed document on grease-proof paper of the Imperial German Government impressively recalled the epoch of slavery during the 19th century, a period firmly connected to professional ivory hunting. Tremendous Arabic trading caravans, with hundreds of porters carrying merchandise on their heads – like rolls of cloth, little barrels of black powder and tons of cheap glass beads – penetrated the interior to barter for ivory and slaves. Porters were the only means of transportation as the use of wagons pulled by oxen, horses, mules or donkeys was made impossible by the tsetse fly.

The traders ventured far beyond Lake Nyasa and Lake Tanganyika and penetrated deep into the Congo, their routes revealed by bush tracks with mango trees growing along them from the discarded pips. The use of Kiswaheli (the coastal lingua franca of East Africa) in the far interior, remind one of these long-forgotten caravan routes which often bypassed unfriendly tribes in search of fertile and well-settled areas, as the question of feeding hundreds of porters was an essential requirement.

Kiswaheli was imported into the African interior by these intrepid travellers and, some years ago, I was able to settle a dispute at Kinshasa airport in the Congo between an English speaking African from Zimbabwe and a French speaking customs officer. As the customs officer understood Kiswaheli, in which I was fluent, I was able to translate what the Zimbabwean was saying to him.

In the eastern Congo, a Belgian traveller once met the infamous Tippu Tib returning home with 3 000 porters, personal staff, 10 concubines and 2 000 elephant tusks. His one and only wife (as a Muslim he could have had four), looked after his palace in Zanzibar while he was away.

Most of the Muslim men I knew had four wives, except my Muslim confidant, Nasoro Mmeta, who only had one. I once asked him why he had only one wife, to which he replied, "One quarrelsome woman is quite enough for me!"

When out in the bush it was always a pleasant surprise to come to settlements which had mango trees during the harvest time. Apart from the fact that the ripening fruit attracts elephants from far and wide, they are delicious. Mangos, by the way, originated from India and were introduced by the Arabs.

In the middle of the 19th century, Zanzibar was the main trading centre for the 'white and black gold of Africa', which meant 'ivory and African slaves'. About 15 000 slaves were brought to Zanzibar every year, mainly to be sold to Arabia, Persia and India, the rest were used on the island itself and on French-owned Mauritius for work in the clove plantations.

Slaves were obtained by robbery or bartering with native chiefs who were keen to capitalize on the prisoners taken during the ongoing tribal wars. That such a state of permanent instability and violence was finally terminated by what is today the heavily condemned 'colonial times' needs to be mentioned, and it should not be forgotten that Africa owes the cultivation of maize and cassava – today the staple foods of many millions of Africa's inhabitants – to the slave trade, which makes the argument rather complex!

The ivory was obtained mainly from professional African elephant hunters whose activities were greatly improved by what were then 'modern firearms'. Black powder muzzle-loaders became increasingly available to these hunters and, long before the well-armed and efficient white nimrods like Bell, Neumann and Sutherland made their appearance, Zanzibar annually exported about 180 000 kilograms of ivory.

*Perfect for a frontal brain shot*

## Chapter Seven

# Potent Medicine
## The Polo Peppermint

I must say a few words about the Swiss Capucin Missionaries of the Kilombero valley, all very helpful and hospitable people and mostly keen hunters as well. They made an unforgettable sight when hunting. They often wore a pith helmet on their heads, a beard reaching down to their belts, a long, grey cassock and a rifle slung across their backs while riding one of those old but reliable motorcycles, like the BSA or Norton and roaring along the bush tracks leaving a long trail of dust behind them.

One of them, the rather short Father Ambrosius, was stationed in Utengule, a lonely mission in the upper Ulanga valley. From afar one could see the small church built on top of a pyramid-like inselberg, which reminded me of an idyll in the Berner Oberland.

Once again I had spent the night there, this time with my colleague, Gil Child. For breakfast, as always, we had a soup plate full of fresh, cold milk and we were just about to leave when a wedding party came out of the church, the African bride and groom beaming with happiness. Heaven knows where they obtained their white and black dresses, probably a loan from the parish which perhaps they kept to encourage church weddings.

Opposite the radiant couple were the family and numerous guests who were also in their Sunday best – multi-coloured cloaks and shawls – and in a cheerful mood. This was suddenly interrupted by the loud wailing of a baby, who was quickly silenced when given to the bride. Without hesitation, she pulled a large breast out of her bodice and fed it, nowadays a not too unusual scene but then, over 40 years ago, it was rather amusing to see, at least for us Europeans.

During a Sunday mass in the rainy season, when the game sometimes moved close to the mission, an African shyly approached the altar to whisper something into the priest's ear, whereupon Father

Ambrosius interrupted the service by ordering his believers to say a rosary while he disappeared into the sacristy. A few minutes later the loud bang of a rifle shot interrupted the prayers and, a few minutes later, Father Ambrosius returned and finished mass without any comment.

After benediction, the congregation left to find a dead buffalo lying a hundred metres from the window of the sacristy. I don't think the priest mentioned having asked for the assistance of the Holy Ghost although I am sure that his faithful flock would have believed him if he had. Instead he had relied on the efficiency of his trusted 9.3x62 Mauser rifle.

Such a wonderful and unequalled story I, of course, do not have. But I did once shoot a good buffalo, although not in my Sunday best but in my long, white nightshirt and slippers. It was not all that far from the Utengule. I was on my way to do some control work when the incident happened.

To begin with I had shot a big zebra stallion which, in that particular locality, have very narrow skin-markings like the Grevy's zebra from northern Kenya. As I wanted to preserve its skin, I camped on the spot to get the skinning and salting properly done and, to escape my skinners' noise, I slept a hundred or so metres from their camp. Being the dry season there was no need for a tent and I slept under my mosquito net.

Shortly after first light I awoke and, there, not more than 30 metres away, stood two, huge buffalo bulls in the morning mist staring at the strange, white apparition under the mosquito net. While they hesitantly walked on, I carefully slipped out of my blanket, took hold of my 9.3x64 Frankonia Mauser loaded with 19-gram soft-nose bullets and followed the beasts as they moved away from me. I stopped behind a solitary tree and, as if by command, the two bulls also stopped, turned around and looked back at me. One of them fell dead to my shot.

I had to wake up my skinners who had not heard the shot because they had gorged themselves on zebra meat until the early morning. Although the buffalo had been stone dead for quite a while, one of my Muslims kicked the carcass and caused it to wobble slightly which he took as an indication that the beast was actually still alive and he cut its throat, thus complying with the Muslim law of Halaal – the bleeding of an animal before it can be eaten. After cutting it up and loading the quarters onto my Land Rover, we set off and, in the late afternoon, reached the starting point for our foot safari in

*The 'night-gown' buffalo*

the Kilombero valley. We parked the Land Rover in the nearby village of Madabadaba Mafinji and I spent the night in a rondavel (a round hut with a corrugated iron roof), built at the edge of the wilderness by the Government for travelling officials.

I had hardly unpacked my belongings when a very dignified, long-bearded, old man walked towards us, his long, white robe reaching down to his feet and the richly embroidered cap identifying him as a distinguished Muslim. I learned that he was responsible for the cleanliness of the hut and for the supply of water and firewood, for which I had to pay three shillings. He welcomed me in a very friendly manner and respectfully asked what he could do for us.

I asked him if he could arrange 12 porters for me (which he said he could easily do by the following morning), and to look after our cars and trophies while we were away. A little later he came back and asked to speak to me on my own. I sent my staff outside, knowing only too well that they would squat underneath the window with their ears pricked. Without any embarrassment the old man immediately came to the point.

"You Europeans are so wonderful, powerful and skilled beyond compare. You have got everything you want. Your medicines are unsurpassed. Please, you must help me. I am in severe difficulties and in a hopeless situation. I have four wives to till my maize fields and, if they desert me, I will die of starvation. I am an old man and no longer able to fulfil the demands of my wives, which is to sleep with each of them every night. If I cannot do this they will run away. You must help me, Bwana! You surely have got the necessary medicine. I will pay any price!"

I was puzzled and held back a remark about his age. On another occasion I had heard that we Europeans did not have the slightest idea about African potency and, to cover my embarrassment and not put the old man on the spot, I told him I would think about it and asked him to come back in an hour.

What the hell could I do? I didn't have a lion skin. I knew that the skins of snared male lions were treasured as a sheet and rented out for five shillings per night as it was believed that the fabulous virility of the king of the beasts would be passed on to the sex-hungry sleeper. Then I had an idea. I had in my travel bag a packet of 'Polo Peppermints' that I sucked on long marches. I wrapped four of them separately in paper and when the old chap returned, I said with a sad face that I had the appropriate medicine alright but, unfortunately, its price was so high that he surely would not be able to pay.

Expecting him to look glum, I saw his face light up. He could and would pay any price and, after some discussion, I produced the four, tiny packets and declared solemnly that, because he was such a nice, helpful man, I would give him the medicine free of charge. Straightening his bent back he walked out like a youngster, only to return after a short while to ask how he would have to take the medicine. "Only one tablet per night to be swallowed with tea," I told him.

He then disappeared but, the next morning while still dark, I was awakened by a babble of muffled voices and there stood a queue of at least 20 men hoping to get jobs as porters. They were to carry a 40-pound load on their heads for three shillings per day, the only cash available in an area where there was no possibility to earn money and, in addition, the even more tempting prospect of game meat.

Nasoro Mmeta, my headman and gun bearer, undertook the signing on of the 12 porters as well as the distribution of the loads. A typical African palaver which lasted about two hours, with the strongest men always trying to get hold of the smallest load. Then

*A Mpagazi porter*

*A Wapagazi string of porters on a foot safari*

the safari finally got under way and, on the downhill march through the swamps below, I remembered one of the few dry spots available for camping where one night we were attacked by ferocious safari ants that had been attracted by the meat of a puku, a rather localized swamp antelope.

We were aroused by the crashing noises of breaking banana plants. Without torches we had to wait for the morning to follow the marauding elephants that had caused the pandemonium in the night. At daybreak we stalked through the most unpleasant *matete* grass (which grew up to 6 metres in height), with pointed, sharp edged leaves where it was only possible to move along narrow hippo paths pulling the foot carefully out of ankle-deep water at every step to avoid making splashing noises.

The sun transformed the thicket into a hothouse but the sound of movement ahead of us indicated the proximity of the pachyderms. I slowly turned my head and, Mawanda, a quiet and very reliable chap who was directly behind me, understood and gently shook the ashbag. The wind was hardly noticeable and what there was drifted towards us. We squatted down and waited and the grey colour of elephant skin moved slowly across my view to reveal a wrinkled forehead and massive tusks.

It was too good to be shot. An elephant with heavy ivory was not permitted to be shot on control hunting as it had to be conserved for high-paying tourist hunters. Very slowly the bull turned his head toward us. Was the elephant aware of our presence, I wondered? Had we been spotted? I glanced back at Mawanda and hoped that he would keep calm.

Then the bull started to move. Very slowly, almost imperceptibly, the blunt and gleaming tusks came nearer and I slowly raised the muzzle of my .458 while I scrutinized the small, brown eye of the bull. It appeared cold and lifeless without the slightest flicker, almost like a glass eye. Beside my right ear the muzzle of Mawanda's rifle appeared. Inexorably the elephant came closer. Was he really unaware of our presence or would he suddenly charge and be upon us?

When he was less than five metres away, I aimed low down on the trunk at a very unfavourable angle and pressed the trigger. Almost simultaneously there was the deafening roar of Mawanda's rifle and the stopping power of the two heavy bullets threw the mighty colossus sideways into the *matete* grass and down for good. Instantly the remainder of the small herd of bulls broke away with an almost deafening noise, escorted by a white cloud of startled cattle egrets. Altogether we shot seven elephants on this safari, all at ranges of 10 to 15 metres, a task which proved the efficiency of our .458 Winchester Magnums from Frankonia in Germany.

It was only on the walk back to Madabadaba that I suddenly remembered the old man who I had totally forgotten about during the hunt. What excuses could I offer to calm the cheated and surely angry old man? And there he was when we arrived but, instead of a disappointed expression, his whole face was a smile. "Bwana," he began, "your medicine has worked very well indeed and I want to buy your whole supply notwithstanding the price!" I left him some tablets and his gratitude was touching!

How could I have foreseen that, about 30 years later, this funny happening would have a similar amusing end? Attending the 65th birthday of a good friend in Namibia, I was asked at the party he gave to tell the guests about some of my hunting experiences. At first I hesitated in view of the number of ladies present but, at last, I managed to present this 'below-the-belt' story quite well and was pleased that my story was so well received.

*Brian Stronach*

# Chapter Eight

## BRIAN STRONACH
### A COLLEAGUE AND FRIEND

Chief Tsetse Officer, Brian Stronach, of Tabora, was my boss. He was an Irishman of my own age and we got on very well together. He later became game warden of Tabora and finally a colleague at CAWM. He had been in Africa longer than me, spoke fluent Kiswaheli, had studied zoology, and was enthusiastic about nature, the country and its native people and was, contrary to me, a first class wing shot. We undertook many safaris together and I learned a great deal from him.

In 1959, he asked me to participate in a big poaching swoop. He had received information about an illegal tribal hunt in the Buha – a game drive with more than 150 participants armed with muzzle-loaders, spears and bows with poisoned arrows. Unfortunately, the poachers, as so often happened, got wind of our intentions.

In the end, we only managed to arrest a single, black nimrod and to confiscate a speared waterbuck. In the evening, the poacher was questioned in our tent. Brian and I sat on camp chairs with the accused squatting on the ground before us. He was a lean, middle-aged man with the usual black cloak knotted around his shoulder. Beside him stood two game scouts who translated the language of the prisoner into Kiswaheli.

As usual, the suspect knew nothing, had no accomplice, was innocent and had found the waterbuck already dead. But the matter got interesting when we examined the pouch he carried under his left armpit. In it he had witchdoctor's medicines for all sorts of magical cures in the shape of powdery substances – a dried crocodile's gallbladder against evil spirits – and ointments to cure snakebites, malarial fever and several other maladies that humans are prone to in the wilds.

Finally, Kitambi, one of the scouts, pulled out a little parcel tied with string which caused the prisoner to become very agitated and he tried to snatch it from the guard. Kitambi unfolded the dirty paper but shut it again quickly, turned up his nose and returned the obviously embarrassing parcel to the pouch. On Brian's prompt questioning the scout replied, "Oh, it is nothing." Well, that was it for the moment, the men were dismissed and our cook served supper.

Having eaten, Brian sent again for Kitambi and demanded. "Come on, out with it. What was in that paper?" Kitambi now declared with a malicious smirk. "Sir, in the paper is the blood of his wife, dried menstrual fluid prepared by a witchdoctor. That is the very best and infallible charm for his safety and for which he would have had to pay a high price to the witchdoctor."

One day we visited a Wanyamwezi chief in the Wembere-Steppe to the north-west of Tabora, a chap Brian knew very well. He was a jovial, friendly and well-fed gentleman who welcomed us with dignity while seated on a beautifully carved, wooden, easy chair. After the usual polite greetings, Brian could not stop himself from making an impulsive remark on the many wives he had in the crowded courtyard. "They are," the old rascal replied, "the wives of those of my subjects who are late in paying their taxes. It is a very efficient method of making them pay." Very efficient indeed, I thought!

In those days the Thomson's gazelle on the Wembere plains were of great interest to me as they did not occur on my hunting grounds to the south. They were incredibly shy and, when they heard a car approaching, immediately fled. But we soon noticed that they did not mind pedestrians such as herdsmen tending cattle.

Walking upright, I managed an easy approach on a herd and, before they became restless, I made my tracker lie down crossways in front of me so I could rest my rifle across his back and shoot from a prone position. Using this rest, I was able to take a good ram. On another occasion, while stalking a bachelor herd with Brian, they ran across our front in full flight at about 80 metres. The first shot from my open-sighted 9.3x62 was a miss but the second bullet took a buck in the shoulder while it was high in the air, bringing the animal down in a cloud of dust.

Brian commented, "Anno, you shoot running tommies with a rifle as though you were shooting hares with a shotgun." High praise indeed from Brian!

## Chapter Nine

# From Bynes Kilanga to Martha Gelhorn

One of my duties as a field officer was to pay the wages of our tsetse staff. I took a voucher from head office in Tabora to the revenue officer in Kigoma or Kibondo at the end of each month and received a huge amount of shillings to pay out to the names on my list. The shillings in those days were copper coins with a hole in the middle so they could be threaded on a string. As the men I had to deal with were mostly illiterate, their receipt of payment was by a thumbprint with the aid of an inkpad. It sounds very easy to accomplish but it was not. Two messengers had to hold the man's wrist and thumb to make sure that the print was pressed into the right line of the ruled sheet.

The Arab or Indian duka owners – a duka being a shop in the bush – always turned up on pay-days hoping to recover some of the debts owed to them. The most persistent offender was Bynes Kilanga, an elderly man, unequalled in the bush but who, between safaris, was hardly ever sober. None of the other workers had more bushcraft or could chop out tusks better than he did. For many years, he had been a gun bearer for John Basil-Reel, a famous old hunter who, up to World War II, operated from Tanga on foot as he could not drive a car. He shot the Maasailand record elephant which had tusks that weighed 168 and 160 pounds aside and the tusks had been removed, unblemished, by Bynes.

To my great regret I had to dismiss him one day due to shortness of funds, a fact he calmly accepted with the fatalistic remark, "It is willed by God." He was paid off and received a bus ticket to his home in Tabora, which was a journey of 560 kilometres but I soon heard that the twice weekly bus had left without him. An Indian duka owner and a policeman had waited in vain for him at the bus station but Bynes had just disappeared.

*Manyara buffalo*

When Brian Stronach was promoted to Game Warden, Tabora, I went with him on a reconnaissance safari lasting several days through the forests and Moyowasi swamps, from Kibondo to Tabora, an all but impossible task by car during the rains. It was now, however, the dry season and our journey developed into a fantastic trip although our two vehicles, a Land Rover and a Bedford lorry, were sometimes covered with tsetse flies. Owing to the lack of water, we saw little game before approaching the Moyowasi swamps but, from then on, we increasingly saw topi, Lichtenstein's hartebeest, zebra and some sable that stepped only hesitantly aside at our approach as they were not used to cars and humans.

And then, late one afternoon, we came upon a herd of buffalo moving slowly across a wide, open slope in ever increasing numbers till they grew into an endless mass of black. "They are like ants," said one of the astonished game scouts. They were impossible to count but we estimated that there must have been about 3000 individuals in the herd. They were most probably a temporary congregation of several herds. We watched in awe, not thinking of doing any shooting as we had shot an eland the day before but also, to be honest, because we saw no bull with more than a 45-inch horn-spread amongst them.

*A good buffalo with a 45-inch spread, but young*

I can only remember one similar situation and that was years later during our college Christmas holidays when hunting with Pat Hemingway. We were at the end of Lake Manyara, well concealed behind a termite mound, from where we watched the exodus of more than 800 buffalo out of the national park. The wind was perfect and they presented themselves in an ideal position, slowly moving in a single file, at an easy shooting distance. We knew that the world record *Syncerus caffer* came from Manyara but we only spotted one bull that was worth looking at. Pat, whose turn it was to shoot, let him go because the bull's soft, hairy boss indicated he was only about five years of age.

Weeks later, this same bull was bagged by Flight-Captain Heinz Baumgart on the adjacent farm of Georg Damm. It had a spread of 46 inches, a wonderful curl and its soft boss could easily be 'fixed' back home by the taxidermist. The German, Georg Damm, was a good friend of President Julius Nyerere and an extremely hospitable man. Georg owned the 20 000 hectare Manyara Estate adjacent to the national park, which had 4 000 head of cattle on it but very many more head of game. Although Georg had gained incredible experience in decades of farm work from Namibia to Ethiopia, he met a typical African fate in 1974. On a night before pay-day, burglars broke into his house and cut his and his young wife's

*The current world record buffalo, also from Lake Manyara, measuring an unbelievable 62¾ inches, photographed 6 months before his natural death*

throats as he was thought to have a large sum of money in the house.

Martha Gelhorn, Pat's 59-year-old stepmother and his father's third wife, was our guest on the abovementioned Christmas safari. While we hunted, she sat reading in camp and rarely accompanied us on our long walk and stalk hunts. When tired, Aunty Marthy, as we called her, could become awkward. Once she made a series of nasty comments about Germans but Pat, obviously feeling embarrassed, stopped her with a sharp remark. She was, however, a character to be reckoned with. She had lived through the Spanish Civil War and, in World War II, was a courageous and fearless, frontline newspaper reporter. Later she wrote a very successful book on her experiences entitled, *The Face of War*. Tough as the old girl was, Pat had thoughtfully obtained an unusual comfort for her personal use – a collapsible toilet with a disposable bag for which we had cut a private 'alcove' in a nearby dense thorn bush.

On the second or third day of our safari, when we were driving slowly along at walking speed, the game scout knocked on the Land

*Mature 49 inch buffalo taken in the Manyara area by G. Dierking, guided by the author*

Rover cab's roof. In front of us we saw a lonely hiker walking along with hardly any kit. It was Bynes who, in anticipation of what to expect at the bus station, had thrown away his expensive ticket and set off on foot, sleeping at night in the top of a tree if there were lions around and living on some provisions he had brought along as well as wild mushrooms and wild honey.

Grinning broadly, he climbed onto the back of our vehicle and we took him with us. Two years later he died of abdominal cancer. Good old Bynes. Liquor was his downfall but it should be mentioned that, posthumously, he received a comical honour which could have easily caused a political stir.

Mr Jacobs, our Goanese clerk in Mweka, was always good for a joke and he asked me for a print of a photo I had taken some years before of a big, male baboon I had shot in a millet field. As a visual memento to Bynes, he imposed Bynes' villainous face, wearing a mischievous smirk, just above the body of the baboon. This picture was framed and hung in the very place in Mweka's head office where the portrait of State President Nyerere had previously hung. Then one day we had a completely unexpected visit from a cabinet minister who came to honour the college with his visit.

When the minister's visit was over, our principal, Dr Lamprey, showed him out and absent-mindedly took him through the head office. The high-ranking guest stopped dead and silently scrutinized the picture before walking to his car. There was, however, no reaction whatsoever but heaven knows how some scatter-brained white man would have behaved in such an event!

*The portrait of Bynes and the baboon hanging in Mweka's head office*

## Chapter Ten

# Ugolo and Pombe

While stationed at Kibondo, which is at an elevation of almost 1500 metres, we considered ourselves to be the highest officials in Tanzania. Our district commissioner was Derek Quinland, a charming Scot who frequently invited me over for a sundowner which usually ended up with him falling asleep. His early drowsiness might have been a reason why his attractive, young wife, Mawa, started having an affair with a lonely, young tobacco officer. Tragically it ended with the unhappy beau shooting himself and the marriage being dissolved – a colonial fate!

Derek was genuinely interested in my work and very helpful due to his tremendous experience as an administrator. From his highly fascinating stories, here is just one which is so typical of the African mentality of half a century ago.

Sometime in March 1959, while checking the records in the control book of the Native Authority Court in Kakonko, Derek's attention was attracted to the following entry: 1. Adultery with the neighbour's wife = 20 shillings fine; 2. Theft of a goat = 70 shillings fine; 3. Contempt of Court = 200 shillings fine.

Derek intervened and questioned the case. The highly indignant African judge reported that during the court session, a boorish and insolent bush-dweller had entered the court room with an '*ugolo* stick' in his nose, which the judge considered an incredible cheek and contempt of court.

*Ugolo* is the name of a very popular snuff which comes in the form of a stick. The normal way of using it is to grind some up in the palm of the hand which is then sniffed into the nose. By coming to court with a stick of it pushed up one nostril, the impudent fellow had violated the dignity of the court. Derek adjusted the fine downwards with an absolute lack of understanding on the part of his

African subordinate.

Derek had not known that smoking and snuffing in someone else's or in a public room was regarded in African culture as the depth of impertinence.

In addition to my duties as a tsetse officer, I was once asked to replace the settlement officer while he was on leave and to look into the unhygienic situation of a settlement near the Burundi border from where increasing occurrences of intestinal diseases had been reported. I was to find that, because of the lack of any hygienic provisions, the inhabitants just squatted down beside their huts. So I held a meeting with the inhabitants assisted by two messengers from the Boma Kibondo who translated my Kiswaheli into Kiha. It began with a long, tiring palaver ending with the willingness of the inhabitants to construct a covered pit at a distance of 30 metres from the huts. This was to be filled in and another constructed when required. Led by the local headman, I inspected the well-dug earth closets six weeks later and was pleased to be able to report the proper execution of my order to the district commissioner.

*Derek Quinland, the D.C. of Kibondo, 1958, in his gala uniform*

I had a gruelling experience once when driving along the main road in the Buha Highlands. I was stopped by an African policeman who asked me to help Bwana Engels with a case he was conducting in a nearby village. George Engels was a German Jew and the chief constable of Kasulu. He was a good friend of mine who never showed the slightest feeling of resentment towards me although the Holocaust was well remembered.

In a courtyard between three huts he was questioning a handcuffed man who had obviously been horribly beaten up and he asked me if I had room in my Land Rover to transport two corpses to Kasulu. Fortunately, I did not have to rely on a white lie as my vehicle was fully occupied.

A short distance from us, a group of silent men sat besides two heaps covered by a tarpaulin, the bodies of the father- and mother-in-law of the culprit who had killed them while drunk. He had then cut off their sexual attributes and was frying them over a fire when the outraged neighbours overpowered him after a fight, which accounted for the man's wounds. I wrote to my parents to tell them that alcoholism hangs like the Sword of Damocles over this wonderful country.

I really had to smile when, many years later, I read a book written by a German *Schutztruppenkommandeur* (commander of a colonial force), in 1898. According to him, it was not unusual for a lieutenant, whose Zulu company should have been on duty, to report that the company was unable to turn out due to drunkenness. At the beginning of the German colonial era, Zulus from South Africa were recruited as askaris.

Whenever I look at one of my best buffalo trophies, I see in my mind the pleasant face of Daniel Otim who was present when I shot the bull near Oldonyo Sambu, in South Maasailand. Otim was a very good student at Mweka, a pleasant fellow and a first class hunter. After his exam he became game warden of Tororo, in Uganda, where he made a mistake that cost him his life. He stopped to help a child that had run into his car and was lynched by a drunken mob.

When driving through villages one had to be extremely careful to avoid drunkards and, in case of an accident, not to stop to help. Instead, one had to drive on to the next police station to report the accident.

Even years ago, serious drinking could trigger off the most gruesome vengeance for the most trifling cause. In 1957, when calling at the police station in Kibondo for a new ammunition permit, the Indian commissioner pointed at an inconspicuous man who was the picture of misery. He had just turned himself in after having

*Waha drinking 'pombe' (local beer)*

killed six people the night before. One was his mother who he had not recognized in the dark. He had stabbed them all with his assegai.

Arson was and still is a popular way to get rid of people. Not far from where my daughter lives in the Transvaal in South Africa, an African's hut was set on fire by a lightning strike and he was burned to death. To find the 'culprit' who had 'directed' the lightning onto his hut, the villagers called in a witchdoctor to investigate and, after sniffing about and consulting his oracles by throwing some bones on the ground, he pointed at some unfortunate villager who he accused of being responsible.

Shortly afterwards the hut burned down in which the innocent man was sleeping. His door had been wired closed from the outside so he could not escape and he was burned to death. Of interest was that the rest of the inhabitants of his village were convinced that he was the guilty person who had sent the bolt of lightning and had been quite rightly punished.

## Chapter Eleven

# LEOPARDS AND CROCODILES

While I did not have much contact with lions in western and southern Tanzania where they were rare, and I only once took part in the slaying of an old and starving man-eater, I frequently met with leopards. These are to me the most beautiful members of the big cat family and, for their size and weight, the most dangerous animals on four legs. When a wounded leopard is followed, it will charge in almost every case, coming like a bolt of lightning without giving any prior warning. The leopard often jumps on the hunter, knocks him down, then bites his face and digs its claws into his neck, chest and belly and it is recommended to have a thick sweater knotted around the neck when following them. The hunter should also use the rifle that he is used to.

A huge leopard was shot and wounded by a hunter from the Rhineland and, within a few weeks after being wounded, the leopard had put two, seasoned, white hunters and a tracker in hospital before it was finally killed by a ranger from the game department. The trackers, who had accompanied the white hunter and his client on the hunt when the leopard was wounded, were convinced that the disaster was triggered because the client had shot a hyena before the leopard. The hyena was regarded as the epitome of uncanny and abhorrent magic.

A client of the Kenyan white hunter, Tony Allen, shot a leopard from a blind with his .300 Weatherby Magnum but, to their astonishment, the cat was not killed on the spot by the ultra-high velocity bullet. Possibly, because the client closed his eyes as he pulled the trigger against the .300 Weatherby's horrendous recoil, the bullet hit the leopard in the belly and it jumped off the bait into the reeds.

On the follow-up, Tony walked in front with the client and the tracker while the client's friend, who had come as a non-hunting companion, brought up the rear. They left the reeds and followed the leopard's tracks into the riverine forest and had not gone far when they heard yells from the companion. The hunters turned quickly only to see the leopard jumping away from the man and back into thick cover. The man had been bitten severely on his face and neck and his abdomen had been ripped open by the leopard's claws.

He was given first aid in camp and then driven to Kibondo Hospital where the doctor who attended to him described him as lucky because, with the wounds he had, he could easily have been killed. I found it interesting that the leopard had let the first three men pass and then attacked the man at the back!

In February 1960, an old African couple was spending the night at Nyaviumbu, sharing a somewhat decayed stable with some sheep and goats. Around midnight, a leopard broke through the thatched roof and killed one of the sheep then, in a leopard's instinctive bloodlust, it raged around biting whatever it could grab. When the neighbours arrived, the surviving animals had broken through the mud wall and the leopard had departed with them but they found the woman unconscious and almost scalped while her husband, who had been severely mauled, had already left for the next world. Aided by two game scouts, I tried for three weeks to destroy the culprit with trap-guns and sitting in hides at baits but all my efforts were in vain. Interestingly, the local villagers believed the leopard was the transmogrified spirit of a departed relative of someone in the village that had come back to earth to seek revenge on those he thought had wronged him in life.

One night a leopard attacked and killed one of the village dogs and, thinking it might be the same leopard I had been trying to shoot, I decided to bait for it and sit in a hide. We cut an opening in some thick bush using long thatching grass for cover and drove a peg in the ground, twelve metres in front of our hide, to which we tied a white goat which we chose for better visibility in the dark.

Around 4 o'clock in the afternoon, Nasoro Mmeta and I sat on comfortable camp chairs in our blind. On my knees, due to the lack of a scoped rifle, lay my double-barrelled shotgun loaded with SSG buckshot. The sun was just going down when excited calls could be heard a few hundred metres upstream. Nasoro, who understood Kiha, told me that the leopard had just killed a goat. Now what? What should we do? We had a short discussion then Nasoro

*Killer leopard*

shouted over to them that they should chase the leopard away and take the goat. We decide to sit till midnight.

The sun had hardly gone down behind the hills of Urundi before the short twilight passed rapidly into darkness. Hardly able to see the goat, I was thinking that, in a few more minutes, it would be impossible to shoot without the spotlight when, soundless and with lightening speed, the leopard came like a rocket, running low to the ground. Within what seemed like seconds, the leopard was standing over the prey he had instantly killed. He was standing side on and, with the bead of my shotgun's foresight scarcely visible, I pressed the trigger of the choke barrel and the leopard collapsed to the shot.

On another occasion while on elephant control with the students of CAWM on the farm of Prince Bernhard of the Netherlands, the *Shamba la kingi* as it was called by the locals, the South African farm manager complained about a leopard killing his goats. This was a most welcome opportunity for Gil Child to demonstrate his ability in catching predators with traps but the cat would not cooperate and killed more goats.

One dark night we were trying to shoot some bush pigs that were destroying the crops and we soon had four lionesses in the beam of our spotlight which were valuable allies against the pigs. Then, at about 80 metres distance, we saw a pair of gleaming eyes. I looked through the binoculars.

"It's a leopard," I whispered.

"That's no leopard," Gil whispered back. "It's a reedbuck."

"Then shoot it," I whispered again. "We need one of those for the museum."

Gil fired and there were no more gleaming eyes to be seen so the driver, Mohamed, started the engine and drove the Land Rover forward. "It must have been about here," he said as he stopped.

In the grass to the right we saw a movement and Gil, who was standing on the back, switched on his head-lamp. "I'll get your reedbuck for you," he said as he clambered down.

"Not so fast," I replied. "For heaven's sake take the shotgun!"

Gil took the gun and walked a few steps forward and then gave a great leap backward as he fired the shotgun in front of his feet and a snarling growl was cut short by the shot. Gil grasped the tail and dragged the leopard to the car.

That again was typical of Gil, a very good shot and sportsman but not an enthusiastic hunter. One of his passions was motorboats and, when a safari went through an area with rivers and lakes, he brought a boat on the back of a Unimog. It was of good use on Lake Manyara and for elephant control along the Kilombero river. On sandbanks and lagoons we often saw hippos but seldom the already over-hunted crocodiles.

One morning Gil and I chugged leisurely along on a 'recce' downstream when we passed an eight-foot croc, surprisingly lying motionless on a sandbank as we passed it. After about 80 metres, Gil turned the boat around and went back while I, with both elbows resting on my knees, sat astride the wooden seat in the prow with my .30-06 Woodsmaster at the ready. The croc continued to lie unmoved and, as the crosshairs of my scope settled on the brain, I squeezed the trigger. The reptile somersaulted backwards and then splashed back into the water.

Gil opened the throttle wide and raced towards it. "Hold my legs," he said as we reached the place where the croc had disappeared into the water and, with that, he plunged his head and the upper part of his body under the surface. In a few seconds he came up again holding the tail of the lifeless croc.

Many authors allege that crocodiles are responsible for the most human losses in Africa. After stopping the shooting of them for expensive, leather goods in many parts of the continent and the

*Feeding time for crocodiles in Burkina Faso*

subsequent introduction of crocodile farms, their numbers have recovered, although it is only in reserves that you may come upon the real monsters. I know that the official record of a croc taken in 1997, at Chewore, on the Zimbabwean side of the Zambezi, had a length of 17 feet 3 inches. I recently saw a croc of a size in the Okavango that left me speechless. I will not hazard a guess at its length. That reptile in the Okavango appeared to me like an archaic dragon, a Leviathan of really prehistoric dimensions. Nothing in the world would have persuaded me to wash my feet in its vicinity.

When on safari in February 2002 in Burkina Faso with my friend, Marc, I was astonished to find that they were protected there and even considered to be 'holy animals'. I could not believe my eyes when I saw women with their children washing in a dam and two fishermen up to their hips in water while, right between them, the noses of some crocs had surfaced!

Near Ougadougu we visited the Mare aux Caimans Sacres de Bazaule. On being called by a cheerful lad swinging three chickens around his head, about 15 crocs left the water and waddled onto the land to be fed quietly together, without haste, on the chickens we had bought for them at 40 cents each. We approached to about one metre and one of our guides even took a seat astride the longest which was about three metres in length. We didn't see any larger crocs but I did wonder whether they were still 'holy' when they grew larger.

*Pat Hemingway (left) and Reinhard Voigt with Pat's kudu*

## Chapter Twelve

# TANDALA
## THE LOVE OF MY LIFE

I wrote the following impressions after I had bagged my first *tandala*, this being the melodious Kiswaheli name for the greater kudu, on the Ruaha river, in Tanganyika, 45 years ago: "... and I didn't know what to admire first: its enormous body weighing about 600 pounds and, despite its bulk, not missing the graceful charm of the antelope, a combination of elegance, beauty and masculine strength. Or those magnificent horns twisted in tight curls and with their length of 53 inches – a real trophy".

An opinion not at all influenced by Ernest Hemingway who, in his book, *Green Hills of Africa*, was equally obsessed with the "Grey Ghost of the Bush", as was his son, Patrick. Yet Patrick, despite all his years as a white hunter in East Africa, only shot his first kudu, in 1979, in Namibia, when I took him stalking on Reinhard Voigt's farm near Windhoek. In East Africa it was always a problem to bag a good greater kudu. They are said to have never recovered from the disastrous rinderpest epidemic of 1896. Even in the days when it was relatively easy to collect the Big Five during a normal hunt of three weeks, the taking of a greater kudu was considered to be the culmination of the classical safari.

The greater kudu was a rarity in the hunting concessions of the safari firms, being restricted to the almost inaccessible and heavily wooded inselbergs of Maasailand and, in 1963 and '64, at the height of the safari trade in Kenya, there were officially only five greater kudu shot in comparison with 179 lesser kudu. Hunters unfamiliar with the behaviour of kudu were defeated by their extraordinary shyness and caution and the fantastic sense of hearing this striped thicket dweller developed. Sudan game warden, A. L. Butler, a keen kudu hunter from the last century, speculated on whether the proverbial shyness of old bulls may not only result

*A trophy kudu measuring 65⅜ inches, hunted by HRH Prince Abdorezza of Iran in the Northern Province of South Africa, 1995*

from experience but also from an increased sensitivity of hearing caused by sound waves led down the horn spirals to those large, funnel shaped ears.

I shot three greater kudu in Tanzania, each a great moment in my life. And more than once I passed up a good buffalo so as not to frighten a kudu which, of course, I did not get in the end.

My third kudu I took quite easily and purely by chance on the way home from a control hunt. It was late afternoon. My long line of porters was loaded with tusks, tails and ears (the latter which we kept for leather) of five or six elephants we had shot on control. As usual I brought up the rear, carrying my .300 Winchester Magnum. We crossed a range of low hills in typical kudu habitat when a premonition urged me to go to the front of the line which had just entered a ravine. On either side were huge rocks and, on the burnt bottom of the gorge, were tall brachystegia trees with freshly sprouted foliage glowing in the most striking colours. In the midst of this unique scenery there walked, slowly and majestically, a huge kudu bull with long, spreading horns, its transparent mane below the neck gleaming against the setting sun like a golden fleece.

This unexpected event formed the worthy end to a remarkable day's hunting. The day had begun with a close-quarter stalk on a herd of elephant. Suddenly, with a mighty roar, not 2 metres above my head, a big leopard jumped off a thick branch it had been concealed on.

*Trophies bring memories back to life - the author with his 'almost' world record, 2003*

## Chapter Thirteen

# Almost a World Record

In March 1960 I had to cut a Land Rover track through the forest, the direction having been previously chosen by Issa, my tsetse assistant, who, aided by a compass, marked trees with his panga every 50 metres. A few days later I inspected the proposed trail by following Issa's marks and I failed to see the next mark as it was blocked by a Lichtenstein's hartebeest which we might easily have overlooked in the high grass.

Owing to the rains and the difficult hunting conditions we were always short of meat, so I reached behind me, took my 7x64 magazine rifle from my gun bearer and fired at the shoulder of the solitary male showing just above the grass. The buck went down at once but soon got up as its spine was only nicked. A second shot luckily got the already running antelope down for good. I instructed one of my men to take the head home where my old factotum, Hassani, boiled and cleaned it. Having forgotten the skull for quite a while, I finally remembered to fetch my tape out of the cupboard and, for many years, it was number eight in Rowland Ward's *Records of Big Game*! Today, 40 years later, it has gone down to rank as number 34 – indicating the fast development of trophy hunting as well as the growing affluence of sport hunters.

I give as a classic example the way in which the world record greater kudu, one of the most coveted trophies of Africa, was obtained. In 1916, a South African non-hunter, J.C. Rous, was urged by friends to participate in an enormous game drive with 500 beaters near Lydenburg in the Transvaal. He borrowed a .22 Savage High Power with which he very luckily hit a kudu bull in the heart. It had 69¼-inch horns and was the new world record. They were only beaten half a century later by a longer pair of horns from a pick-up killed by lions on the Save river in Mozambique.

*Thomson's gazelle – a big ram*

In conclusion, a rather funny event occurred that caused some mischievous smiles among fellow hunters. A certain white hunter, known for his boastful and bragging manner, had promised to find his American client a record oryx. In due course the sportsman gut-shot the coveted beast and they had to chase it with their Land Rover. Eventually they came upon what they thought was the wounded animal and succeeded in shooting it but, when they approached the dead beast with their tape measure at the ready, they found their record oryx had transmogrified into a Maasai donkey. The white hunter had a double-barrelled name, let's call him Burton-Miller. He was henceforth nicknamed by his colleagues 'Punda Miller', punda being the Kiswaheli word for a donkey.

Like other game animals of the arid thorn bush, independent of open water, oryx are very tough beasts and, when shot with a light rifle like a 7x64 or a .30-06, they are easily lost. To my shame, this is what happened with my biggest oryx. What saddened me, was not only the loss of that wonderful trophy but, more so, the painful memory of my bad shooting which I hope was soon compensated for by merciful lions or wild dogs.

Bushbuck are the smallest member of the spiralled horned antelopes. Strictly habitat oriented, they are rather localized and, if one knows their whereabouts, can be quite easily hunted despite their shyness. I had already bagged the two to which I was entitled on my general game licence when, one morning on the Greater Ruaha river, I came upon the biggest bushbuck I had seen so far. Unable to shoot it, I made use of the opportunity to take some photos from fairly close range and in good light.

Snapshots are perhaps more valuable than certain trophies for I had not seen any good bushbuck pictures from the wilds. In my youthful imagination I was convinced I would cause a sensation with these photos in sportsmen's magazines. Understandably, I could hardly wait to collect the photos from the drugstore in Iringa, however, the sloppily inserted film was unexposed! Breathless with shock and disappointment, I stumbled out of the shop feeling the unhappiest person in the world.

*My safari kitchen, in aid of unhampered mobility " free from the tyranny of possessions..."*

## Chapter Fourteen

# Buchengera and Lake Tanga

From 1950 to 1960, Lake Tanga to the east of Kibondo was known for big elephants. Shielded as it was by dense, waterless bush and only accessible under the guidance of local honey gatherers, it took a 10-hour, cross-country drive, mostly in low gear, to get there. Beside me in the Land Rover was Buchengera, a modest, middle-aged inhabitant of Buha, considered to be one of the most frequently convicted poachers and famous as one of the best trackers in western Tanzania. It was the end of September 1959, and the beginning of my 14 days local leave, which I was actually supposed to spend with my family on the beaches of the Indian Ocean. Instead, I tormented three Africans and myself by struggling through endless bush under the smoke filled haze of the late dry season, the heat turning the vertical rays of a merciless sun into molten lead.

Spring was approaching and, with it, the unfolding display of the filigree-like foliage of the brachystegia trees. The colours varied from bright emerald green to fiery copper and purple red. Like a radiator mascot on the bonnet of my vehicle, Oresti, a young African tracker, guided me through the grass by signalling any hidden obstacles like ant-bear or warthog holes, fallen logs or, most important, the termite mounds that were as hard as concrete and capable of denting the oil sump of the car.

Despite a lavish spraying of DDT on the outside of the car, the tsetse flies were prolific and the inmates of the vehicle were under constant attack. We saw no game the whole day except for a few common duiker and a young buffalo bull which I almost rammed as he rose unexpectedly from the grass, causing Oresti to give a gigantic leap backwards. At last, with the sun almost down, we descended through small hills and, instead of an idyllic, blue lake, we arrived at a rather sobering dirty sheet of water, about an acre in extent, which was the legendary Lake Tanga.

From the elevated campsite, which was a bed with mosquito net and a simple kitchen, I was able to observe the water with its surrounding open flats from a safe distance. At dawn I looked through my binoculars for the signs of nightly visitors in the form of elephant droppings which we later examined when circling the water looking for tracks. As there was nothing worthwhile to follow up and we didn't want to cause a disturbance by driving around needlessly, I lazed away the whole day sweating in the sparse shade of the camp. I dozed off every so often only to be roused by the shrill call of the red-chested cuckoo which was common there.

Towards evening the scene livened up. Solitary, old, buffalo bulls came to drink or take a mud bath and, once, a bachelor herd of eight bulls came in followed by roan antelope, a few jet-black sable and the inevitable baboons. But no elephant.

It was still twilight on the third morning when Buchengera woke me to say there was a big elephant but it had only one tusk. Buchengera looked at me while I assessed it through the binoculars but I finally refused. I estimated the tusk to weigh about 130 pounds, equal in weight to a normal 65 pound aside and I decided to let it go as there were still a few days left to hunt.

At the end of the open flats surrounding the drying out waterhole I could see the bleached white skull of the 145 pounder that had been shot 2 years previously under guidance of Buchengera by an old British colonial officer who shot on the morning after, when they cut out the tusks, a second elephant coming to the water, another hundred pounder!

But the big, single tusker remained the only decent elephant we encountered. It was like a curse and my Africans were convinced that my medicine was useless. And this was especially so when, on the way home, I topped the luckless safari by wounding a sable. Finding the animal lying on the ground after following the short blood trail, I aimed for the neck to administer the *coup de grace*. The sable's head dropped just as I fired and my bullet struck the base of the one horn which flew off through the air!

An American writer once wrote words to the following effect: "Every day you get your beating, no matter in what way."

# Chapter Fifteen

## Unakula kila siku?
### Do you eat every day?

From Mweka I occasionally drove across the Sanya plains (with its big Thomson's gazelles), through the not very deep Kikuletwa river and then up the Lelatema mountains right into the Maasai *nyika* for a weekend hunt. This countryside was made known a hundred years ago by the German wildlife photographer, Schillings, in his book, *Under the Spell of Elelesho* (the dominant bush in Maasailand).

One can hardly imagine another landscape conveying such a feeling of dreary loneliness and melancholy as this slightly undulating, greenish grey carpet of low acacias and commiphora thorns, its wilderness being topped by isolated, blue inselbergs whose euphonic and sonorous names alone can cause wanderlust. There I hunted for lesser kudu which, because of its graceful body and splendidly marked coat, is also called the 'Apollo of the Antelopes'. I was probably too choosy for I never encountered a worthwhile head there.

But there was another encounter I will not forget. On these short safaris I took only one of my men along to watch camp and I always hunted alone as I could not get lost due to some well-known hills. On that particular morning I had already seen gerenuk, Grant's gazelle and oryx when, crossing a big, open flat I saw, in the distance, a lone man coming straight towards me. I noticed through my binoculars that the tall chap, who was unusually sturdy for a Maasai, carried a gun on a sling across his back.

As he seemed physically superior and rather self-confident, I thought it better to dispense with my duty of asking him for his licence. Instead we met in a friendly manner with the usual Maasai greeting of *Soba*. He then scrutinized me from head to toe and asked in Kiswaheli, "Do you eat every day?"

*Lesser kudu*

Rather dumbfounded I replied, "Yes, of course."

"No, not me," he said, "Only every second or sometimes even third day".

I stopped myself from mentioning the nutritious diet of sour milk and clotted cow's blood that enabled the Maasai to trot along on their stork-like legs for hours. He then began to discuss the hunting of his favourite game, which was the eland, while I gave preference to the gerenuk, whose long, giraffe-like neck enabled it to reach up and select the choicest leaves that, in my opinion, gave the delicate aroma to its flesh.

After a short and casual chat we parted and I never learned his whereabouts – a rare sight among the otherwise non-hunting Maasai cattle-breeders.

The important role of the Maasai in game preservation can be derived from comparable figures compiled by the then Director of National Parks, Mr. S.P. Molloy, after an investigation some 40 years ago. In the east of the Serengeti (Maasailand), there were hardly any problems except the spearing of occasional rhino and lion, while in Sukumaland (to the west), about 120 000 game animals were snared annually and another 30 000 killed with poisoned arrows. What cruelty to animals could have been avoided by well managed cropping schemes! But admittedly, then as today, even on a much smaller scale, they were impossible to organize.

In the western Serengeti I witnessed a small herd of wildebeest passing rather hurriedly through a small acacia forest when, all of a sudden, some bushes and trees began to shake wildly. A number of the unfortunate animals had run into snares and, as it was impossible to free them without risking serious injury, we had to shoot eight or ten of the beasts. The whole three or four acres had been efficiently blocked with snares.

I camped at the foot of a hill with Gil Child who spoke some Kimaasai, when we were visited by three, youngish Maasai warriors who asked for medicine. Some time earlier I had purchased from the Christian Bookshop, the only bookstore in Moshi, an old German map from colonial times and I now tried to show off my knowledge by naming a couple of nearby inselbergs. The three lads seemed baffled, putting their heads together and telling Gil that I must be a very old man as the names mentioned were used during the time of their grandfathers only.

I once dined with a well-dressed, Maasai chief from Kenya in one of the best hotels in Nairobi. When I asked him during our conversation why he did not sell some of his numerous cattle, he replied, "What shall I do with all the money?" He then explained to me some of the customs and traditions of his tribe and that the warriors

*A Maasai Moran with his ostrich feather headgear and a shield made from buffalo hide*

*Southern Maasailand (Umba Plains)*

would retire at the age of 30.

"And what do they do then?" I asked.

"Eat meat," was his reply.

He declared proudly that they practised polygamy, a remark that reminded me of a quotation of the great elephant hunter, James Sutherland: "At 30 or 40, the African is an old man and then his chief worry will be to keep his women from committing adultery. Possibly the hardest task of his life in which he invariably will fail."

Once, after an instructive and very wearing excursion with the students of the college, which took us all day along the forested slopes of Ngorongoro Crater, we finally saw the Maasai village where our unimogs were waiting to take us back to camp. The anticipation of the end of our strenuous tour put some life into my protégés, causing one fellow from Uganda to cockily exclaim, "Lets get down there to start work on the Maasai girls."

One of his Maasai comrades reacted angrily. "Don t kid yourself. You being uncircumcised, you won't have the slightest chance with our girls!"

*Nyala*

## Chapter Sixteen

# Beautiful Antelope

During the last decades, some of the most coveted and exclusive trophy animals have lost their mysterious aura due to effective protection, which has led to the successful increase of species that, in the past, had been almost eradicated.

In the 1960s, the common nyala, one of the most beautiful antelopes, was thought to be very rare. Along the Shire river in Malawi I considered myself very lucky to be able to observe these highly protected animals and I never thought it possible that, 20 years later, many would be on offer on the game farms of Natal, with only the expensive trophy fees being an indication of their legendary rareness of the past.

*The essence of grace amongst the African antelope, the common nyala*

With many of these rarities the exact 'knowing where' was important, as was the case when I hunted the sitatunga. In Kibondo, where I was stationed, a European had once caused a sensation by shooting a female, as even a female sitatunga was considered to be an unusual bag. Since then they had almost been wiped out in that area as they lived in narrow papyrus habitats where they were prone to being snared, which was why sitatunga had not been much on my mind. This changed when I visited the White Fathers mission in Ujiji. The priests occupied the old German boma and there, hanging on the wall, I saw two sitatunga skulls with horns. According to the inscription on the skulls, they had been collected by German colonial officers around 1910 in the Luiche swamps bordering Lake Tanganyika.

To my great surprise, I was in due course ordered to check the tsetse fly situation on the Luiche river but my initial euphoria vanished when I came to the conclusion that the invisible animal with elongated hooves, so well adapted to the swampy ground, fully deserved the reputation of unbelievable shyness. Despite all my efforts I never managed to intercept them when they returned from the bean fields of the locals into the vast and impenetrable papyrus thickets bordering the lake where they hid during the day. On the sandy edges of the lagoons, the unmistakable tracks of the animals were clearly imprinted but they seemed to be entirely nocturnal and I almost despaired, trying to console myself by thinking that I was lucky to have at least seen their tracks.

After 10 or so futile outings, my last hunting day arrived and, around noon, I was to be picked up by my tsetse crew in the government launch. Before dawn, with the aid of a torch, I reached the hide I had erected at the beginning of the hunt in a place that offered a good line of fire, with a wide view across an open glade surrounded by high papyrus. The first chirps of smaller birds began to interrupt the silence, the prelude to the mighty concerto of an unbelievable avifauna that, within a few minutes, would fill the air while the form of the landscape slowly grew in the predawn light and large flocks of waterfowl flew like black veils across the cloudless sky.

As eager as all the days before, I searched the edges of the reed and papyrus thickets through my binoculars, knowing that it was my last day in sitatunga country. But nothing happened. Disappointed, I finally began my retreat, again and again turning round to look back for the last time – when I was shocked! At the

*The only sitatunga I encountered in East Africa*

edge of the papyrus there stood a sitatunga gazing at me!

Despite a distance of more than 150 metres, my binoculars clearly showed the massive neck with its long hair, the small head under lyre shaped horns with ivory coloured tips and the dark and shaggy body. I was furious that I had left my hide too early. And then he turned. I let the binoculars drop on the strap around my neck and brought my rifle up. The bull did not return to the cover he could have reached with one step but walked towards a papyrus thicket. Now or never! I bent down and ran forward to gain a better shooting position but the buck began to trot into high grass that almost covered it. With only the white dorsal stripe showing, I quickly swung my rifle up, fired and heard the bullet strike.

I ran forward and, with a few jumps over the wet spots, I reached the buck. My bullet had taken it high in the neck and hit the spine, which was perhaps the luckiest shot of my life as it was the only sitatunga I ever saw in East Africa.

Years later I came across them again in the Caprivi Strip and the Okavango swamps where organized safaris from dugout canoes were quite successful. But I never expected that they could be watched on the swampy clearings in the rain forests of Gabon and Congo Brazzaville's National Parks, sometimes with bongos and even gorillas sitting up to their bellies in the lukewarm water.

*The pygmy guide with my blue duiker*

I also never thought that, during a holiday in Kribi in the Cameroons, I would have the chance to hunt them, although for only one day with a long, single-barrelled shotgun belonging to my pygmy guide. Sitatunga must have been rather common for, after stalking for an hour through the very, wet rain forest, we found the unmistakable, elongated spoor but failed to come up with them which, of course, would have been asking rather a lot. All the same, I managed to shoot a blue duiker.

On the way back to his settlement, I once again enjoyed the funny, Pidgin English of my guide. He suddenly stopped, pointed upwards into the high canopy and, at my inquiring glance, said, "Beef in tree." This meant 'meat in the tree', which is their term for monkeys.

*Taken by surprise, this puff-adder goes into defensive position*

# Chapter Seventeen

## TAZAMA NYOKA!
### ATTENTION - SNAKE!

*Tazama nyoka* was the warning cry which could be heard quite often, especially during the rains, from the tracker or guide leading a foot safari or hunting party when coming across a snake on the footpath. Newcomers to the colonial service, so it was said, were advised to always let an African walk in front in the bush as his education was far less expensive than that of an expatriate. Nevertheless, this joke had a more serious background. From childhood, the rural African is used to paying attention to the ground on which he walks and will discover in time the sluggish puff-adder lying on the path, while the more dangerous cobras and mambas react to the vibration of the ground caused by his footsteps and slither away. In fact, in the whole of Africa, more human beings are bitten by puff-adders than by all the other poisonous snakes put together.

I came in contact with snakes almost daily when, in order to develop new settlement areas, I supervised the deforestation clearings to eliminate the breeding habitat of the tsetse fly. These clearings were carried out at the beginning of the dry season when there was still enough unburnt grass around to build makeshift shelters for 200 or more men, working under orders of their chief, to claim new, fly-free small holdings. Their job was to ring-bark all the trees with their slim axes up to about one metre from the ground while there was still sap in the bark. This caused the canopy to die which meant there was no dampness on the ground due to lack of shade which, in turn, prevented the fly from breeding.

In the morning I paced out the stretch of the daily workload, its end being acoustically marked by two drummers. The pay of the village labourers consisted of a bowl of coarse salt per day and I don't remember how many hundredweights I had to bring by lorry to the bush. One or two supervisors were armed with single-barrelled shotguns to shoot snakes that had taken refuge in treetops.

They were mostly harmless species as less than one third of African snakes are considered to be poisonous but, occasionally, there were also cobras, boomslangs and black and green mambas. The game warden and snake expert, Constantin Ionides, supplied institutes all over the world with live snakes for the production of snakebite serum. These were all caught near Newala in southern Tanzania and included 3 000 green mambas without a single accident in the thickly leafed mango trees where, during the ripening season, hundreds of small boys climbed about. Ionides, an Englishman of Greek origin (and known in the game department as The Greek), was not only a world-renowned herpetologist but a great hunter too. He was also a cranky eccentric who is said to have written in his will that his funeral should be left to the hyenas.

Gil Child, then the game warden of Arusha, was confronted with the aggressiveness of the black mamba. On one safari, his cook and the cook's wife were bitten by a mating couple of black mambas that they surprised in an old safari kitchen near Lake Manyara. An hour later they were both dead.

To take a snakebite serum along one needed to have a fridge. The white hunters, of course, with appropriate transport facilities, had such comforts for the necessary cold drinks to pep up their clients after the hunt but who in those days could afford such a luxury on a game control safari?

While on a college safari in the Umba steppe, we had just pitched camp when an excited student reported that a big black mamba had been seen disappearing into a patch of bush between the porters' open tents. This was a dangerous situation because the consequences could be terrible if such a deadly snake should slide across the sleepers on the ground during the night.

After a short discussion, a number of Africans armed with clubs formed a circle of about 15 metres diameter around the snake's hideout, leaving a small opening where I squatted on my shooting stick with a .410 loaded with dust shot on my lap. The dry foliage of the bush inside the circle was set alight and, about 10 minutes later, there was a sudden yell opposite me. Orumoi, a tall Maasai, gave a jump and struck down with his club. The next instant the mamba came towards me with slightly inflated neck, the forepart of its body upright and the head erect. At a range of two metres I pressed the trigger and the slim body lashed helplessly on the ground before the men finished the drama.

A rare and rather localized snake I came across was Storm's water cobra from Lake Tanganyika. It averaged over two metres in length and lived on small fish. It was fascinating to watch its elegant swimming in the crystal clear water of the lake but my crew was utterly horrified when I tried to paddle alongside it with the boat. It was supposed to be very poisonous but, luckily, we had no chance to test it.

On Lake Tanganyika I also experienced the only snake bite during all the years I was in Africa – which fortunately was not on me! While searching for pupae of the tsetse species *Glossina palpalis*, Hassani, who was walking in front of me, suddenly jumped high up into the air and shouted, "I have been bitten by a mamba!" He ran a few metres, staggered and vomited, his eyes suddenly bloodshot. And then he fell on the ground unconscious.

After removing his puttees, we discovered two blood-drops near the shinbone of one of the legs. I immediately took off my shirt, threw it over to Nasoro, telling him to ligature the leg while I ran to the camp. I was back half an hour later with the serum I had stored in my kitbag and the medical assistant who, by chance, was staying in our camp. I was flabbergasted. Hassani, the snake's victim, lay there as though he was dead and Nasoro had ligatured the wrong leg!

Without hesitation, the medical assistant very professionally injected the – as I thought – life-saving serum from my South African snakebite outfit. It was only later that I learned that, by applying the improperly stored serum, which should only be kept in a fridge, we could have easily caused more damage than the snake. During my absence, Nasoro had done something very sensible. The old bushwhacker had cautiously crept back to the place where Hassani had been bitten, found the coiled up snake and beheaded it with his panga. It was about 35-inches long, emerald-green in colour and by no means was it a mamba!

We took it with Hassani to the hospital at Kigoma which we reached after two hours travel by boat. Our patient had by now regained consciousness and was shivering violently, his teeth chattering in spite of the terrible heat. The Italian doctor, Ugo Fornari, who by the way had helped my second daughter to see the light of day at Ujiji, compared the dead snake with a show board depicting all the dangerous snakes, then declared with a large smile that we could pick up the patient in two days time. The snake turned out to be a slightly poisonous Rhombic night adder, a 'back-fanged' snake, meaning its fangs were situated at the back of its jaw and injected only a small quantity of poison when striking in self-defence.

The black-necked spitting cobras were common. In defence, they are able to spray their venom quite efficiently up to three metres away into the eyes of an intruder, causing immense pain and temporary – or even sometimes permanent – blindness, if not treated quickly and properly. One night, Musa, one of my tsetse-boys, received a full load into his eyes. Fortunately the hospital was nearby and he was released the next day. In the bush, an immediate rinsing with water or milk will help and, if necessary, one has to urinate into the affected eyes which are held open by an assistant. In any case, once back from the safari a physician should be consulted.

Last but not least, I have a quite amusing snake tale to tell that I heard from my friend, Gisbert Poensgen, who was the German ambassador in Lagos, Nigeria. At an evening party in the park-like garden of the embassy, his houseboy announced the presence of a poisonous snake, whereupon Gisbert ordered him to kill it. After a while the poor chap returned trembling with fear to report in classical Pidgin English: "Him not agree to die!"

Snakes have always fascinated me, these relicts of primeval times, their presence being an indication of untouched and virgin habitats.

## Chapter Eighteen

# KUCHINJA
## HALAAL

*Kuchinja* in Kiswaheli means the imperative act of religious throat cutting, which the Arabs call 'Halaal'. According to the Koran, a live and conscious animal must have its throat cut to allow its soul to escape with the flowing blood. The soul must not be consumed by human beings and, if an animal is not Halaal, it may not be eaten. If the animal was still alive after being shot this was what I considered to be a barbaric act of cruelty that I was unable to prevent when hunting with Muslims but one that I tried to avoid whenever possible. 'Unclean animals' like warthogs and bush pigs were not butchered or eaten and the same applied to elephants as it was impossible to cut their throats.

*Warthog - an 'unclean animal'*

*A buffalo stampede resulted in a buffalo double...*

A funny episode once happened regarding *Kuchinja* near Mikumi National Park. When returning to camp with two Unimogs full of students, we saw two wildebeest bulls standing in the open woodland. Being short of meat, I stopped the cars and stalked the bulls from behind the big trunk of an *Erythrina abyssinica* – a beautiful, solitary tree. At a range of about 200 metres, I fired broadside at one of the animals which fell on the spot to my 9.3x64 Brenneke TUG bullet. The students on the back of the Unimogs had, up to then, been exemplary in their silence but now applauded loudly while the driver, Mohamed, with an assistant, came running to do the *Kuchinja*. But the animal kicked so wildly that the two Muslims did not dare attempt to hold the head.

Meanwhile, Charles Ntkaonja, a student from Malawi, joined them to try to hold the beast by the horns but, instead of approaching from behind, Charles very stupidly came from the front and was seen instantly by the wounded animal. It got up very quickly and charged Charles who now ran for his life, the sharp points of his pursuer's horns almost touching his behind. As I didn't dare shoot, the chase went on for at least 50 metres before the wildebeest turned to run away. With Charles out of the line of fire, I could finish

*...and a non-halaal, but delicious meal*

off his would-be assassin but, even after the beast collapsed, Charles would not stop running, to the great amusement of all the spectators.

*Elephant hunting provided the local population generously with meat*

# Chapter Nineteen

# PRIMITIVE WAYS

While the dry climate of South Africa enables hunters to prepare their beloved biltong (jerky), the high humidity of East Africa does not allow a similar method for preserving meat. Normally the European hunters shot their meat for the pot on the last two days of the safari so that they could put it in the deep freeze at home. The Africans, however, relied on the smoking of elephant and buffalo meat which, when cut in thin strips, dried quickly, lost much of its weight and so was less bulky to carry. In this way the majority of big game shot on control was utilized by the locals and was considered by the Government to be compensation for the damage caused to their fields.

A horrible story of meat preservation, almost unbelievable to 'civilized' Europeans, was told to me by my late friend Jaques Guin, of Garoua, a very trustworthy and credible white hunter of the Cameroons who specialized in guiding for giant eland. Just after the last war he hunted elephant in Liberia where, in those days, these pachyderms were still plentiful. Camping in the rain forest at the last village that he could reach by canoe, he became well-acquainted with the very primitive Africans who he engaged as guides.

On one occasion, a lad with white chalk marks on his otherwise naked body, attracted his attention. When these signs multiplied, Jaques became inquisitive and one of his men explained to him that the young man had been cured by the local witchdoctor of an illness. As he was too poor to pay for the successful treatment, he automatically became the property of his benefactor but, after a while, the witchdoctor got tired of feeding his useless slave and decided to capitalize by slaughtering him! Although highly illegal, cannibalism was still prevalent in the West African forests and, well aware of the quick putrefaction under the equatorial climate, the sly witchdoctor had decided to commercialize his victim by 'advance booking'. When totally sold and portioned alive, the pitiful youngster would be slaughtered.

Here I had to interrupt Jaques's story. I commented that, being well aware of his fate, the doomed man could easily have escaped by running away through the forest – full of drinking water and food in the form of fruit, small animals and fish – before reaching safety somewhere far away. "No," Jaques replied, "this victim of black magic was so convinced of the unlimited power of the sorcerer that he helplessly gave in with no will of his own."

The signs of white chalk marks on the body demarcating hands, legs, feet, pieces of the back or belly increased gradually until one day Jaques returned from a hunt and the man had disappeared. Similar occurrences in the Congo are related in *Hunter*, J.A. Hunter's well-known book.

A very primitive and cruel way of storing meat was practised during my days when several animals were caught simultaneously in pits. Their legs were broken or tendons hamstrung and the unhappy beasts kept alive until required for food.

In Maasailand we occasionally found snare-lines installed by Ndorobos. Long thorn fences were constructed around waterholes or across migration routes where oryx, gerenuk, gazelles or lesser kudu were carefully driven towards open gaps blocked with wire snares. The Ndorobo also dug very cleverly disguised pits for buffalo, rhino and bushbuck in the Hygenia forest. I once nearly fell into such a trap that I only noticed at the very last moment.

The Ndorobos were the most backward people I met in Tanzania and, during my time there, they were the only tribe that the Government allowed to hunt with poisoned arrows. They were in loose contact with the Maasai with whom they bartered honey for milk. Originally Maasai themselves, they lost their cattle during the rinderpest outbreak of 1896 and only survived by hunting. Today they still roam the countryside as hunters and gatherers.

Their name is derived from the Maasai words *El dorobo*, meaning 'the poor'. However, in Kiswaheli, *ndorobo* also means a tsetse fly and, during my time as a tsetse officer, I was known among the Africans as 'Bwana Ndorobo' and it was up to me to decide whether this designation was related to my continuous shortage of money

*Waha hunters, having killed a hartebeest with their muzzle-loader*

or to the dangerous insect.

The poison for their arrows is a thick black paste smeared for a length of up to four inches behind the arrow head. The bow hunters produce this extract by boiling the wood and roots of the Acocanthera tree, a process during which no women are allowed in the vicinity and none of the chaps involved could have had sex before starting with the preparation.

When hunting in Somalia I heard a rather similar story. To guarantee the much dreaded efficiency of the arrow poison, nobody who suffered from syphilis or gonorrhoea was allowed to participate in its production.

I never found the well-hidden grass-shelters of the Wandorobo and rarely met them. Even in the driest country they found the smallest catchments of rain water in rocks or hollows of baobab trees. Captain Moritz Merker, the leading research authority on the Maasai in the old German East Africa, wrote: "Regarding their patience, endurance, bushcraft and hunting skill there could be hardly a European nimrod to compete with these primitive men."

In the forests of western Tanzania I frequently met bow hunters with poisoned arrows. They preserved the poison behind the arrowhead by carefully protecting it with green leaves against deterioration from moisture and sunshine.

In 1960, I was summoned to the police station at Kibondo where two Waha hunters had handed themselves over. As *corpora delicti* they handed over two, big bundles of grass and leaves, the one containing the head of a buffalo that was smelling and crawling with maggots and the other, no less smelly, being the chopped off head of a man.

While following a buffalo that had been wounded the day before, the hunters came up to the still alive beast that charged immediately. Several hunters loosed their arrows at it and, in the ensuing mêlée, the buffalo knocked down one of the hunters who was then hit by an arrow. He and the buffalo both died.

The paste prepared from the bark of the Acocanthera tree is extremely dangerous and even a graze from an arrow can be deadly. Time of death depends on the part of the body hit. The meat starved hunters cut a bit of flesh away from where the arrow penetrated and only people with open wounds in the mouths or ulcers in the digestive tract were endangered.

Serengeti game warden, Myles Turner, reported the case of a poacher who stumbled while running away and inadvertently stuck a poisoned arrow into his thigh. Although immediately rushed to hospital, he died 40 minutes later while still on the transport vehicle.

# Chapter Twenty

# Life-Savers

## The Ashbag and the Mosquito Net

For hunting in the tropics I would like to name two absolutely indispensable items of equipment.

Firstly, the ashbag is a small porous cloth bag filled with wood ash from the campfire. Even when lightly shaken, the ash emitted shows the direction in which the wind is blowing. I never approached big game without an ashbag. Some people try to determine the wind direction by kicking up dust, which is mostly impossible during the rains.

Secondly, the mosquito net, which is not only an essential malaria prophylactic but, without it, especially in the rainy season, sleep at night was impossible due to the clouds of anopheles mosquitoes and other midges which attacked with a nerve-racking buzzing. Only too well do I remember the nights during my sitatunga hunt on the Luiche river in Tanzania when, with growing darkness, myriads of these pests surged against my mosquito net under which I had to undress for the night and then spray the intruders that managed to slip in the moment I crept under it.

I fully agree with the legendary General von Lettow-Vorbeck who once stated: "Nobody who has not yet spent a night in the heart of tropical swamps is able to imagine the multitude of insects one is exposed to. When my officers were without a net, they would rather sleep immersed up to their necks in water and risk possible attacks from crocodiles, leeches or snakes, than be at the mercy of these pests."

During my time, mosquito proof tents were already available on the market but I found that they did not provide enough air circulation on hot and muggy nights. Besides, they were too bulky to be carried on foot safaris. But may I mention that I never got malaria, which was probably due to my strict and regular intake of an effective

*A woman in the last stage of sleeping sickness*

prophylactic which in those days was Daraprim, with one tablet taken per week.

The word 'mosquito' is Spanish for 'small fly'. They are not partial to smoke which is the reason why the bush Africans, who do not have nets, sleep close to the fire that they keep burning all night. Travellers in the 19th century remarked that the beehive-like huts of the Zulus in South Africa did not have a smoke outlet yet their inhabitants kept fires burning inside all night, which is perhaps the explanation why the tribe settled successfully in fever-stricken countries. In the early years, without an adequate medical cure, malaria prevented white settlement in parts of South Africa. The Kruger National Park and other wilderness areas owe their intact eco-systems to the anopheles mosquito which, like the tsetse fly, is responsible for the preservation of vast stretches of big game habitat in East and Central Africa.

I don't know how many thousands of bites – red hot burning stings but, fortunately, not long-lasting like those of wasps or bees – I received from my 'employers', the tsetse species *Glossina morsitans* and *Glossina palpalis* but I was unbelievably lucky to have been spared from infection! My successor in the tsetse department, who was a very health-conscious chap and extremely worried about infection, got sleeping sickness after only three months. Experts

*Miombo*

say that only one in a thousand flies carries the disease.

Effective prophylactics, like those against malaria, were not available for sleeping sickness while insect-repellents caused too much sweating during the hot hours of the day. But always after returning from the bush, blood-slides were taken that showed under the microscope if there was any infection of the dreaded trypanosoma and, fortunately, the initial stages of the illness were comparatively easy to deal with.

We had about 100 cases every year of the human sleeping sickness which were treated in Kibondo Hospital by Dr Isidor Laufer, the sleeping sickness specialist of the Government. But it was much harder to cope with the *nagana* that affected the animals. Considering the vastness of the endless tsetse bush, all domestic animals like cattle, sheep, goats and horses would inevitably be infected after contact with the fly and would invariably die. I think that the only domesticated African species that were immune were the Nubian wild ass and the West African guinea-fowl. Indigenous game was immune except for those animals that were kept in captivity as, after a time, they could lose their immunity to the illness.

When sleeping in the open under my mosquito net, I was hardly ever afraid of lions although I always had my loaded 9.3 Mauser lying beside me which, admittedly, was not a very cosy bed fellow. One morning along the Greater Ruaha river, my horrified employees showed me a lion track that passed my bed at a distance of five metres. They were, of course, convinced that I had a first class witchdoctor's brew to keep myself safe from them.

Myles Turner, who lived in the Serengeti for many years among lions, firmly believed in the protective effect of a mosquito net. Once on the Tarangire river, for several hours, I lay during a pitch-black night between two obviously competing lions calling incessantly to each other. They were so close that I thought the sound waves of their roars must vibrate the net and I did not have much choice but to lie quietly, pull the blanket over my head and eventually fall asleep. Being in a game reserve, I was, of course, unarmed!

When I woke up towards morning, I wondered why everything was so quiet – and gloried in the fact that I was still alive! I would be lying, however, if I claimed that I had not been frightened during that night.

Once the mosquito net did let me down, although in this particular case I was not attacked by lions but by *siafu*, those terrible red safari ants that can even put elephants to flight. Somehow they found a way to creep under my net and chased me out of bed. Stark naked I had no alternative but to call loudly for my men who pulled about 20 of these horrible, voracious, little creatures off of my skin on which they had taken a strong hold with their sharp mandibles. The rest of the night I spent, not very comfortably, in the cab of my Land Rover.

In the morning the ants had disappeared but my experience of a few hours before reminded me of known incidents where *siafu* had eaten hens in their chicken-coop down to the bones and even killed babies in the cradle. I had triggered the above attack through my own fault. I had noticed a few *siafu* in a foxhole not too far from my sleeping place and I committed a fatal mistake. Instead of leaving them undisturbed, I poured some paraffin into the hole and set it alight. Instead of driving the *siafu* away, they took revenge a few hours later!

## Chapter Twenty-one

# Malagarasi Ahoy!

Here is a small episode to boost my own vanity, one of the few 'feelings of success' I achieved without the aid of my African companions. On a foot safari with some 15 porters and 'fly-boys', as the tsetse personnel were called, we had to cross the Malagarasi, a permanent river that, in the 1900s, was famous for its many hippos and crocodiles. Fifty years later most of its dangerous animals had dwindled to only a few survivors, which I didn't mind at all as can be understood from the following.

Arriving from the vast woodland, we reached the Malagarasi's banks opposite a little village of fishermen who we hoped would take us across in their dugout canoes. But alas we received no response from the other side to our calling. The settlement looked deserted with nobody to be seen and the dugouts high up on the banks.

I wondered what was going on. Did they fear a tax collector from the Government or were they just attending a millet beer party elsewhere? As it was not even midday, I did not want to put the tents up and, after some discussion with my guide, I decided to swim across in order to find people to ferry us. This was a task I couldn't expect from the few swimmers among my subordinates who were cautious of possible crocodiles.

The river was in flood, about 150 metres wide and running swiftly. About 10 metres upstream of my proposed landing place, I waded into the brown water then struck out with fast, energetic strokes to swim to the opposite side, carefully avoiding floating tree trunks and uprooted bushes that shot past. I could be sure of the comment of my anxiously watching crew: "What a good witchdoctor's brew the European must have!"

Having landed more or less at the right place, I walked along muddy footpaths, through maize and millet fields to the next huts and was more than pleased to find an old woman. My concern that she might be afraid of being confronted, on her own, for the first time in her life, by an almost naked white man, my only dress being rather tight underpants and plimsolls, were unfounded. She didn't show any surprise or shyness.

After I had uttered the greeting phrases, I asked her if there were any men around. "Yes," she answered, "the men are over there." She then led me for about ten minutes to a group of sinister looking types who soon turned talkative after they realized that I was not a tax collector but just the 'Bwana Ndorobo'.

With two dugouts made from the hollowed out trunks of Borassus palms, each having a paddle and a long bamboo pole to punt with, we managed the crossing without any mishaps although some of my protégés felt nervous, especially poor, old Nasoro Mmeta, who was known to be scared of water and who showed mortal anguish on his ashen face.

It might be worth mentioning that, during this safari at Buhoro, which was an almost forgotten settlement deep in the bush, I came across a young mother who had just given birth to twins. About eight days later, while on the way back, I wanted to take a photograph of the two little ones but, alas, my request was met by an embarrassing silence. At that time I was still unaware of the 'obligatory' practise of many African tribes that killed twins in order to spare the mother's physical strength. About the way they do it I prefer not to tell but who would like to cast the first stone considering the thousands of abortions undertaken at home just for welfare reasons?

## Chapter Twenty-two

# Buffalo from Lake Manyara

"The most beautiful country in the world," as Ernest Hemingway called it, that vast wilderness area which he hunted and wrote about in his book, *The Green Hills of Africa*. In the middle of the geologically significant Rift Valley there lies, shimmering like gleaming silver, the 30-mile long Lake Manyara, surrounded by some of the most famous big game areas on the globe. The lake's name comes from the Maasai word for the very common euphorbia tree that grows there, the *Euphorbia tirucalli*.

One Sunday evening while on that picturesque sheet of water, the outboard engine of our wooden boat went on strike, resulting in an uncomfortable night for Gil, Brian and me, who were all instructors at the CAWM. At dawn I awoke, shivering and stiff and then looked over the rail – and froze. About 80 buffaloes, with only their heads emerging out of the shallow lake, stared at me like sea-monsters, the nearest being only 20 metres away. Safe from lions and insects, they must have spent the night lying there in the water about 100 metres from the shore.

Heaven knows when they came into our vicinity during the night without getting our attention or our scent. However, within seconds, they stormed panic-stricken towards the shore, leaping high out of the water in clouds of spray – a fantastic sight!

As it was, one of us had to undertake the three-hour walk to camp along the shoreline through sand, swamp and forest. I volunteered to go. I walked happily into the bright, morning sunlight with my loaded .300 Winchester on my back, enjoying the sight of numerous shorebirds, waterbuck, impala, reedbuck and wildebeest and was almost led into temptation when, at not more than 40 metres, a tremendous buffalo with a horn-spread of surely 50 inches stood before me. But he and I were still in the national park!

*Lake Manyara – to Hemingway "the most beautiful country in the world"*

Shortly after passing the boundary into the free hunting area, three, old bulls strolled from the lake into the riverine thickets along the shore and I made up my mind to follow them. Not very far from where I expected to find the buffalo I smelt a pungent stench and found the remains of an elephant in a small clearing that had been shot by game scouts on control. And then, suddenly, I saw several sleeping lions that were not more than 20 metres away from me, made conspicuous by the dark patches on the backs of their ears! I counted about a dozen females and big cubs lying in the dry grass, all gorged with the stinking carrion of the rotting elephant carcass and I very carefully retreated, unnoticed by the cats.

In order to reach the lake shore and because of the direction of the wind, I had to walk through the forest which had a layer of dry leaves on the ground. This caused a loud, crackling noise with every step and I knew that the unavoidable noise would be heard by the bulls. I abandoned all hope of a successful hunt but when I came to the edge of the forest I heard a sudden splashing of water. I hurried a few metres forward and clambered up into a small acacia tree from where I had a better view. Two of the buffalo were just disappearing into the thicket with the third following. The bull stopped broadside on for just for a few seconds at about 80 metres. I had no

*Gil Child with a buffalo from Lake Manyara*

time to assess the trophy, though from its body size, it was fully grown.

I managed to pull off a quick shot as the beast jumped into cover, the thump of the bullet telling me that I had scored a hit. Moving forward slowly, I thought I saw a movement near where the buffalo had been standing when I fired, so I moved closer to investigate. And then, just like a mirage, a huge lioness that had obviously also been stalking the buffalo, rose and glared at me. I could do only one thing. Keeping my eyes fixed on her, I retreated slowly with my rifle at the ready. The lioness watched me without moving and, after I had widened the gap, she sank down into the knee-high grass with only her massive, round head showing.

I could not track my buffalo through the thickets of the riverine forest without the help of a tracker. After reaching camp, I returned with a Kenyan Maasai named John Nairi and another student from Uganda who were both experienced hunters. I was sure that if my buffalo was dead, the lions would no longer be at the stinking carcass but, just as on the morning before, all the big carnivores lay close to the elephant, some on their backs with their paws in the air. What a shock!

Not very confident now of finding my buffalo, we searched for blood at the place where the bull had received my bullet but found no signs whatsoever. Then John Nairi went down on his knees and examined almost every centimetre until we reached the edge of the thicket and there he discovered some brown stems that showed blood streaks. The two Africans in front of me froze, holding their rifles at the ready, until one of them pointed with his head and there was a big, black mound behind a tangle of plants. I gave a sigh of relief. In the slanting rays of the morning sun some bluebottle flies were just visible creeping around the blood-soaked entrance wound on the shoulder.

We were surprised to find that the lions had been at the carcass and eaten a little of it. They had, however, scorned the rest of the animal for the time being, preferring instead the tender carrion of the rotting elephant carcass crawling with maggots. The bull's horn-spread was only 42 inches, a bit disappointing but what did it matter in view of the adventure!

## Chapter Twenty-three

# Unimog Causes Irritation

These cross-country vehicles made by Mercedes Benz in Germany were the backbone of the Game Warden Training School at Mweka (CAWM) as 70 percent of the instruction consisted of practical training that was carried out on safari in the bush. Being part of the German Economic Aid Programme and, due to a bilateral agreement, the Unimogs were imported duty free.

Unloaded at the port of Tanga, they were registered and licensed by our English agent at the port. I drove down with our German mechanic, Alfred Schwarzmann (who was in every respect an absolutely top-notch man), over the 380 kilometres of gravel road to the coast to take possession of them. We usually stayed with Oscar Charlton, the tremendously helpful game warden of Tanga. Oscar, a bachelor, was the last white officer to live in a house in what used to be a very quiet residential area but, after the influx of African neighbours, the air was filled, day and night, with the loud, throbbing sounds of portable radios. Perhaps this was one of the reasons for his taking to the bottle as he had a tendency to rely on his almost hourly 'heart starters' as he called them. He had, however, had a shocking war experience, as he only told me very much later.

In 1943, as the navigator of a Lancaster bomber, he was the only survivor out of a crew of seven when they were shot down over the Ruhr and was taken prisoner and sent to the P.O.W. Camp, Stalag 3, in Silesia. From there, he and over 50 of his comrades escaped together through a tunnel dug underneath the fence but, after a short period of freedom in the snow-covered pine forests, they were all caught and Oscar owes his life to the wording of Hitler's and Himmler's orders to shoot all officers involved in this escape.

Oscar was only a sergeant and the wording of the above-

*The mechanic, Alfred Schwarzmann (left), with my hunting client, Klaus von Amsberg, later Prince of the Netherlands, in front of the unimog*

mentioned order saved him from the firing squad. Nevertheless, he was so badly treated by the interrogating Gestapo that he suffered from defective hearing and other permanent disabilities as a result. After the war the British Government compensated him for this with the post of a game warden in East Africa, a job he had passionately longed for.

One day I had to make another visit to Oscar as the German Ambassador, Norbert Berger, had managed to prise another

Unimog out of Bonn which was a welcome addition to our small fleet. On arriving in Tanga, our clearing agent told me, to my astonishment, that the port authorities refused to release the Unimog without the payment of the import duty. After a phone call from Oscar's office to the German embassy in Dar es Salaam, the matter was settled.

The next morning, however, we received the same information as the day before – no Unimog without paying duty. So I again drove to the Custom's House where I managed to see the custom's superintendent, but not before getting past his voluptuous secretary who lolled over her almost empty desk, chewing sugar cane, with her mind in neutral. The man himself was one of those small, lousy, clerk types to be found, irrespective of colour, all over the world. He grunted when I told him that custom's duty was not due in this case but could see that he could not care less about our import arrangements and that he wished only to see the money. A really nasty piece of work!

Leaving Oscar, I drove in a stinking mood back to Kilimanjaro where I moved heaven and earth and, finally, received a verbal release! But … the next morning I received a cable from Tanga: No duty free import of Unimog.

I had had enough! Absolutely fed up, I wrote a very polite letter on my typewriter requesting the Ministry for Natural Resources, our relevant ministry, to ask the Federal Republic of Germany to withdraw their presence in Tanzania. The reason, as I explained, being the obvious unwillingness of the responsible authorities to fulfil the bilateral agreement.

The result of this letter was twofold. We immediately got our Unimog and I received a very brusque and formal letter of caution from our Embassy accusing me of incredibly undiplomatic behaviour towards our honourable counterparts. Without apologizing, I answered that I had lived in this country long enough to know which language to use under these circumstances, a language that our valued counterparts were able to understand. And thereafter there was silence.

How naive I had been in dealing with Prussian bureaucracy. I learned decades later (when a friend told me) that, due to that incident, my name was put on a red list and I was considered to be politically unreliable by our Embassy, although whenever I met one of the embassy members they were as friendly as ever. There is a saying in Germany: Shot through the breast from behind.

*The Kazuramimba elephant, shot with my 9,3x64*

## Chapter Twenty-four

# SAA NGAPI?
## WHAT'S THE TIME?

Early last century, the men in charge of several hundred porters carried a cockerel with them in a basket in order to be woken up in time in the morning. I was without a watch for over four years but, when I was on safari, I did not follow these ancient habits but relied on the early calls of certain birds, like the Scops owl or ground hornbill and orientated myself during the day, just as the natives did, by the sun.

This I owe to the only otter I ever bagged in my life. After being shot in the head with my 9.3, the otter drifted, bottom up, in an enchanted, little lake lined with water lilies, in the Southern Highlands of Tanzania. As there were no waves to wash it up on the bank, I changed into my birthday suit and stepped into the icy cold water to retrieve my rare trophy which was an African spotted-necked otter (*Lutra maculicollis*) but, in my eagerness, I forgot to take off my watch. I didn't bother much as the expensive Swiss chronometer, a wedding present from my father, was supposed to be waterproof but, after about an hour, it stopped.

Africans are fascinated by the watch and, although it is almost a status symbol now, in the very early days it was considered to be some sort of magic. When the German Colonial Officer, Werner von Grawert, became Commissioner of Usumbura, the Africans called him 'Bwana Tik-tik' because he owned a watch.

For many Africans, anything unknown or inexplicable is linked to magic. In June 1960, I shot a crop-raiding elephant on a sisal farm called Kazuramimba, that bordered the central railway line. In the afternoon, while its ivory was being cut out by my men, I went out with a local farmhand to try for one of the roan antelope that were common there. We placed ourselves on top of a big anthill at the end of the sisal fields where the almost endless brachystegia

*A local beauty from Lake Chad*

woodland began.

The sun was nearly down but, instead of the expected roan, a big elephant bull came from behind and almost took us by surprise. I managed to put him down only at the very last moment, at ten metres, with three, quickly fired, heart-shots from my 9.3x64 Brenneke. But, before I could shoot, I first had to open the magazine from underneath to exchange the soft-nose bullets in the rifle for the solid bullets I always carried in my pocket, my ashbag coming out of my pocket with the cartridges. Afterwards, the farmhand told everybody that he had seen with his own eyes how I had drawn my witchdoctor's charm from my pocket, whereupon the elephant had walked right into the line of fire.

The owner of Kazuramimba sisal plantation was a very lonely, elderly Greek, named Kimon Emanuel. During the day he used to sit with his feet up on a swivel chair in the centre of his house that was built on top of a hill and entirely lined with glass. Beside him was a small table with a pair of binoculars and a bottle of whisky and thus he was able to supervise the work routine on the estate under the direction of his manager.

His hospitality was superb and typical of the farmers and missionaries of those days. While there, I was his guest at lunch and supper that was served by his very devoted and smartly dressed, black wife. She did not eat with us and, even when he was on his own, she took her meals separately with the children and the servants. The daughters from their marriage received the best education possible in a convent school near Kigoma.

In my opinion this was a very practical solution for Europeans living alone in the wilderness like Kimon Emanuel. He was well aware, of course, that the English considered him to be 'colour blind' and it was seen as a sign of social decline by the white establishment during colonial times.

It was perhaps the simpler way of life of the Greeks, as well as their participation in hard manual work, that influenced the natives in their classification of mankind, which were Africans, Asians, Europeans and Greeks. The latter, as well as the Italians and Portuguese (because of their darker complexion and black hair), were considered to be different to the white Europeans.

You can find an almost identical assessment in Alfred Brehms, *Travels in the Sudan* 1847-1852. The book contains the statement that, in Karthoum, Greeks were not considered to be Europeans – a view mainly held by the French, English and Turks.

It was remarkable that the integration of American coloureds and blacks coming into the country as Peace Corps workers was not as smooth as expected, at least during my time in Africa. The locals did not accept them as equals and called them 'Negroes'. They found little social contact with Africans and quite often joined the European clubs instead.

*Maasai lion*

## Chapter Twenty-five

# Simba Ananguruma
## A Lion's Roar

Even in the second century A.D., Claudius Ptolemaeus, the well-known geographer of antiquity, characterized his map of Africa south of the Mediterranean coastal belt with the three succinct words: *Hic sunt leones*, meaning 'Here there are lions', a statement that has not lost its meaning for many bush-dwellers even today. *Simba ananguruma* is Kiswaheli for 'a lion's roar', the verb rendering a perfect onomatopoeia of the roaring to which people listen with bated breath in the wilderness at night.

The man-eaters of Tsavo were notorious. The two lions brought the building of the strategically and politically important Uganda Railway to a standstill in 1898. These two man-eaters killed 28 Indians and about 100 Africans employed to construct a bridge across the Tsavo river before they were dealt with by Col. J.H. Patterson, an event that was important enough to be announced by Prime Minister Salisbury in the House of Lords.

Ironically, that famous killer of the two Tsavo man-eaters, who later became a white hunter taking out safari clients, vanished shortly before WW I together with the wife of an American client, who had allegedly committed suicide in the bush. The incident created a lot of suspicion and became the inspiration for one of Ernest Hemingway's most fascinating stories entitled, *The Short Happy Life of Francis Macomber*.

The hunt for a man-eater can become problematical when the finding and killing of it fails and more victims are killed and eaten, for then the superstitious Africans quickly tend to link the failure of the hunters to the dealings of witchdoctors. It was only due to such beliefs that, around 1940, some lions in the Njombe district of Tanzania, an area short of prey animals, were able to kill about 1000 human beings before Game Warden George Rushby and his scouts managed to stop the drama after a long and strenuous endeavour. George, who wrote, *No More The Tusker*, which became a best-seller, gave me detailed information on man-eating in connection with witchcraft and let me look at files of court records of the Singida murder trials. These trials concerned the superstitious fear of an incredibly primitive population, almost still in the medieval stage of development, who were exploited by some very cunning witch-doctors.

These witchdoctors claimed to be the masters and monitoring body of man-eating lions, promising protection for money or carrying out murder 'by lion' for individuals seeking revenge, for 40 shillings each. To carry out such atrocious orders they made use of specially trained 'lion men' who were kept in underground dungeons or hollowed out termite mounds, sometimes for years, unable to stand upright and completely shielded from the outside world. They were poor, mentally disabled creatures who, according to the court files, had been driven out of their minds with drugs. They were fed with meat, honey and mush and, from time to time, supplied with sex partners with which to copulate in a lion-like manner.

Depending on the circumstances and orders, such a *Mtu simba*, as a lion man was called, was led at night on a rope, heavily drugged, to the hut of the victim. Disguised by a lion's mane or monkey skin as a headdress, they wore paw-shaped sandals cut from old motor car tyres and mittens made out of real lion pads complete with claws.

As the heels of the feet of the *Mtu simba* were usually severed, the poor creatures had to move on all fours that left a rather realistic pattern of tracks on the ground. Uttering grunting roars (it was usual to have their vocal cords cut so that they were unable to speak), the assassin rammed a big knife into the heart of his victim, then mutilated the body with his mittens to simulate a lion attack and even devoured some pieces of flesh.

Any witnesses that happened to be present were almost paralysed by horror and all declared that they had seen a lion, a statement of which they themselves were completely convinced. Even officials of the local administration, fearing reprisals from the sorcerers, quite often refrained from passing on suspicious reports to higher authorities.

On one occasion, a game scout returning from a hunt for a man-eater, reported that witchcraft and not a lion was responsible. After

*Mussa Rhajabu (on right) with an eland bull, slaughtered halaal*

arduous enquiries an investigating detective proved that 30 supposed lion kills were actually murders. The whole extent of the horror was brought to light by the facts of a number of murder trials in Singida in 1947, where 27 out of 57 accused were sentenced to death.

The motives for these murders were mostly ridiculous: quarrels over millet beer, disputes among relatives, a desire for revenge for some imagined insult and so on. However, almost none of those trained as M*tu simba* were apprehended. Just before the police operations took place they disappeared without any clues as to their whereabouts!

It was in the ill-famed area of Beni, on the edge of the Central African Rift Valley in the Congo, where, at the beginning of the 1940s, the A*niotos* or leopard men, a secret society shrouded in mystery, killed hundreds of innocent victims. In a similar fashion to the lion men of East Africa, specially chosen youths were trained at isolated localities in the forest where they were turned by unimaginable torture into absolutely spineless creatures. After this preliminary training they had to eat human flesh, dress in tree bark and leopard skins and were forced to kill their own wives or, as they were mostly still unmarried, a member of their family.

They were then given girls and received at their wedding festivities a set of claws made out of wrought iron, which today can be seen on display in the Belgian Africa Museum in Tervueren. Finally, after lots of trouble, the Belgians succeeded in stamping out the plague by hanging many of the culprits who were said to have faced the gallows with an incredible serenity.

Fear and superstition played an important role in the hunting down of the notorious man-eater of Massanza, in 1958, just before I hunted elephants in that area. Even during the spine-chilling end of the tragedy, the lion took three lives within seconds and heavily mauled another victim before Musa Rhajabu killed it as it bit into the muzzle of his rifle by simply pulling the trigger.

After the death of the man-eater, the inhabitants of Massanza deserted the village as they feared the revenge of the lion's ghost. Musa Rhajabu, to whom the Queen awarded the British Empire

*The skull of the old man-eater of Massanza*

Medal, was one of the most noted big game hunters in the game department. I consider myself to be lucky to have had the opportunity to hunt with him.

The old lion's skull, with its worn teeth, was given to me by Brian Stronach as a farewell present when I retired from the Colonial Service. Brian, who was the last European game warden of Tabora, feared that after his departure this unique trophy would land on the rubbish dump. But let me now come to the end of this chapter with an unusual lion experience that sounds like a real hunter's yarn.

Early one morning in 1960, when stalking with my tracker along the grassy Ebanda plain looking for Defassa waterbuck, I was confronted by sudden loud lion roars so close by that I instantly brought my rifle to my shoulder. At about 40 metres distance, a big lioness ran by at speed while uttering a loud, angry roar with every bound. She was being closely chased by four, big, silent baboons with what seemed like fierce determination. With bated breath we watched that fantastic pursuit until they disappeared into the bushes. I have to leave it up to the reader to think of an explanation!

*Eastern Lowland Gorilla, Kahuzi-Biega*

# Chapter Twenty-six

# Lake Tanganyika

A more striking contrast than Lake Tanganyika is hard to imagine when compared to the tiring and monotonous savannah country of the interior during the dry season. Having just climbed the last hills before Ujiji, you are suddenly confronted by the shining, blue waters of Lake Tanganyika beneath you which, after Siberia's Lake Baikal, is the deepest inland water in the world.

About 650 kilometres long and situated in the Central African Rift Valley, Lake Tanganyika represents a type of watershed between West and East African fauna and flora. Unforgettable are the emerald green, forest slopes that fall, without a shoreline, directly into the crystal clear water and the endless surface which stretches towards the green mountains of the Belgian Congo on the far horizon. Little did I know that, 30 years later, my two Tanganyika born daughters and I would meet face to face with the mighty gorillas of Kahuzi-Biega in the Belgian Congo.

My tent stood right in the middle of the Gombe Stream Reserve, later made famous by the well-known scientist, Jane Goodall. Gombe was the most easterly habitat of the chimpanzees in Africa and there I was lucky to take the first photos of the East African chimpanzee species, *Pan troglodytes schweinfurthi*. This was connected with an experience that was to bestow local fame on me in the national press.

Tanganyika Standard, 28 May 1958

"W. Province thief ate a blanket. The first day one blanket was missing. The next evening three more blankets and a coat had been taken from the tent. The Africans in the party, sent by the Tsetse Department to a remote fishing village north of Kigoma to prepare a strip for spraying with insecticide, began to suspect the

> local fishermen.
>
> On the next evening when he returned home, Mr. A. Hecker, in charge of the party, saw a large, male, chimpanzee sitting in a tree thirty metres from his tent. In his mouth he was chewing the corner of a blanket – the mystery was solved. Going closer, Mr. Hecker found the missing coat neatly laid out at the foot of the tree. Two oranges had been removed from the pocket and put neatly side by side on a nearby stone. As for the thief, he slid quietly down the tree and quickly disappeared."

My headquarters in Kigoma could only be reached by boat with an outboard engine, a luxury most of the local fishermen could not afford, although their catch was very much sought after. The sardine-like and sun-dried d*agaa*, as these fish were called, was marketed by rail all over the country. On dark, moonless nights, schools of *dagaa* were attracted by paraffin lanterns fastened to the bow of the fishing vessel and caught in nets; a romantic scene when the many shining paraffin lights could be seen flitting silently over the lake during satin-blue nights.

There was the same procedure nearly every morning. Breakfast in front of my tent in the bright beams of the rising sun, with 10 or 12 children of the tiny fishing village, named Kasakela, silently gazing at me in wonder and with large, round eyes. Then Game Scout Uledi Songoro would arrive, brandishing a stick and shouting furiously, "*Toka, Msungu anakula*!" (Go away, the white man is eating!).

Uledi was retained by the Government in his old age to look after the problem free reserve which was hardly ever troubled by poachers as they were afraid of the chimps. On the steep, wooded slopes there were buffalo, which I stalked and photographed, as well as bushbuck, bush pig, leopard and the Red Colobus monkey.

Uledi had had an interesting life. He had been an askari under the German General von Lettow-Vorbeck and, to impress me, he sang several German military songs and the German National Anthem in Kiswaheli. He was full of praise for his last commander, Hauptmanni Schultz, a well-known, old campaigner of WW I. Uledi proudly displayed old war wounds which nevertheless were dismissed by Nasoro Mmeta as the result of drunken brawls.

From Kigoma I occasionally toured the shoreline of Lake Tanganyika with the Kibisi, a small steamship I could officially hire from the Government. Once I surveyed the well wooded Kungwe

*Aloysi came to a gruesome end...*

Mountains about 100 miles to the south which, from the heavily tsetse-infested banks, rose up to a height of 2480 metres. There were large numbers of chimpanzees there and, although never hunted or disturbed, they were as shy as their relatives in Gombe and I never saw one.

One incident during this boat trip I remember to this day with a certain uneasiness. I noticed that two members of the crew were busy butchering large, carp-like fishes and, when I saw the way these chaps were doing it, I almost got goose pimples. Beginning at the caudal fin of the tail, they cut their very much alive, four kilogram victims along either side of the spine. On seeing this, I immediately grasped their knife and killed the fish with a stab into its brain. I explained to them the unnecessary torture they had inflicted on the helpless creature, to which they replied, "Yes, you are right. We had just not thought about it."

Shortly afterwards, when coming onto the deck again, I saw they were cutting up the second fish in exactly the same manner without having stunned or killed it. They only looked at me and grinned stupidly. I wondered then if it was a question of evolution or the north-south gradient.

There existed an incomprehensible lack of sympathy for the suffering of animals and I feel obliged to mention the killing of leopards caught alive in wooden traps by thrusting the red-hot tip of a spear through the anus to penetrate up into the chest. In this way, the valuable skin was not damaged by a stab wound.

But I also knew a sensitive African, named Mweka Aloysi, who was a skinner and general dogsbody at the CAWM. He could not bear to see an animal suffer and demanded finishing shots when an animal was already as good as dead. It was a tragedy that he met a very gruesome fate because, a few years after I had left Africa, he was found drowned in a cesspit, murdered by rivals as a result of his involvement in the smuggling of semi-precious stones mined in south Maasailand.

# Chapter Twenty-seven

# On Safari in Somalia

In Somalia in 1966, I had to conduct an elephant hunt for the President of the German Parliament, Dr Eugen Gerstenmaier, who was on a state visit in connection with some economic aid programmes. The circumstances were quite amusing because, at the same time, the Cold War was at its peak and a high-ranking Russian official also happened to be in Mogadishu and the two had to be kept apart.

To ensure that this did not happen, the Somalis very cleverly invited Dr Gerstenmaier, whom they knew to be an ardent hunter, to shoot an elephant out in the bush far away from the capital during the days that the Russian was there. In those days there was neither a professional hunter nor a safari organisation in the whole country, so I had to fly in rifles and camping equipment from the College stock.

A Cessna charter plane picked me up at Moshi airport with my full load of hunting and camping equipment and flew me to Kisimaju in the south-eastern corner of that dry country in the Horn of Africa. Before landing, I asked the pilot to fly low-level so I could see what the country was like – it was mainly thorn bush! I was met at the airfield by a dark-coloured, oriental gentlemen, the Minister of Defence and the Governor of the Lower Juba Province, the latter being a very shady character as I was soon to find out. A little later Dr Gerstenmaier arrived in a Government charter plane and, on being introduced to him, his first question was how close we had to approach the elephant before firing. Picturing my air reconnaissance of just half an hour ago, I declared innocently, "Well, about ten metres or so, I should think."

The obviously surprised man just answered "Oh, is that so?"

The German Ambassador who had come with Dr Gerstenmaier

*Dr Eugen Gerstenmaier with his elephant (author on the right)*

took me aside and asked in very stern tones if I was aware of my duty to Germany in being responsible for the safety of such a high representative. What an honour, I thought.

After a two hour drive in Land Rovers along the most awkward bush tracks we arrived at the campsite near a big dam where numbers of cattle and camels were watering. Dr Gerstenmaier was given a rather antiquated caravan to sleep in but the high-ranking guest was almost knocked over backwards by the most ghastly stench imaginable. Obviously the toilet of the domicile, which had been standing in the hot sun, had not been drained for weeks. So my VIP guest got one of the tents I had brought along instead.

During the first three days, our two guides, who fortunately both spoke Kiswaheli, seemed to be disinclined to look for elephant. So instead, Dr Gerstenmaier shot good trophy gerenuk, lesser kudu and warthog. On the morning of the fourth day we drove to a meeting point where our two guides were waiting for us and we followed them on foot. Without them I would have been hopelessly lost in the monotonous vastness of that thick thorn bush. The heat in this sunburnt wilderness was extremely oppressive and much worse than in Tanzania. We had, as it turned out, to march for three hours and I was astonished how well Dr Gerstenmaier withstood the hardship.

On the way we passed two, big trees towering like landmarks above the canopy of the bush and, under each of them, were several Africans that seemed to be waiting for us as they joined our party. The trackers determinedly walked on without following an elephant's track. They eventually stopped, pulled me to the front and pointed. At the end of a narrow opening and in the shade of a big umbrella thorn tree, there stood two elephant bulls. I quickly shook my ashbag to check that the wind was in our favour.

The bigger bull was nearest to us, standing head on at about 30 metres. The chest was covered by a bush but, above it, was the completely clear, massive head which offered a perfect, frontal brain-shot. I indicated a suitable tree to the doctor on which to take a steady aim but, without hesitating, Dr Gerstenmaier shot offhand. My bullet followed almost simultaneously and, with a sigh of relief, I saw the bull collapse in a cloud of dust. I instantly ran forward and fired an insurance shot into its heart.

The bull had spotless ivory weighing about 80 pounds aside. I wondered why some typical, bright reddish, lung blood dripped out of the trunk. On investigation I found that my guest had not aimed for the brain but had shot right through the middle of the bush the bull was standing behind. Luckily it had not been deflected by branches and his .458 solid bullet took the bull in the centre of the chest, which would have been a deadly shot even if I had not intervened.

Unfortunately, the exuberant enthusiasm of the overjoyed hunter soon turned sour. The heat-exhausted man was craving water and, to my great dismay, our uninvited companions had taken it upon themselves to drink our entire supply. I hastily sent two runners back to the cars where two crates of Coca Cola had been kept in reserve, only for them to return empty handed. The Governor of the province had arrived at our cars and, together with his followers, had made short work of all our supplies.

Poor Dr Gerstenmaier was now completely done in and was hardly able to utter, in the most insulting language, the complaint he intended to make to the President of Somalia. We managed to help him to the car and I must honestly say that he really deserved his excellent trophy elephant.

Only a few days later we were again unlucky with our day's food supply. While on a hunting trip we lost the Land Rover that was following us with our provisions for the day but, fortunately, as a

*Ivory transport – no different to 100 years ago*

precaution, I had brought sufficient drinking water with me. While looking for the lost vehicle it began to rain and we got hungry. A short time later we arrived at a small village where we stopped. One of my men went to speak to the inhabitants and, about half an hour later, we were approached by a woman who offered us a freshly killed and grilled lamb which was deliciously tender and very palatable. We had a really notable meal as we sheltered from the pouring rain under the projecting roof of a hut, with me holding the 'sacrificial lamb' and one of the highest representatives of Germany pulling bits of the meat off with his fingers!

An amusing incident occurred one evening when we were returning from the wilderness along one of the rough bush tracks. Some years before, Americans looking for oil had cut many miles of tracks across the country and we used those which were still visible. While driving along we came across a youth who had eloped with his bride-to-be, so we offered them a lift.

Dr Gerstenmaier sat beside me in the cab of the Land Rover while on the open back were two policemen and the well-known Governor who continually lifted the headscarf of the pretty young girl. To my surprise, he asked me whether she would not be something for Mr President, as he addressed Dr Gerstenmaier and suggested I should offer her to him. I, of course, declined to do so, replying that it was up to him to ask Dr Gerstenmaier. After a short discussion he decided that he himself would keep the girl for a couple of days to punish the cheating husband for his illegal abduction without paying *lobola* (her bride-price) to her parents, which would have been in the form of a number of cows.

The happy mood of our group was, alas, shortly interrupted by an incident I accidentally caused. During lunch, when I helped myself to the pepper pot, an otherwise very welcome breeze blew a small cloud of Pili *pili*, the hottest red pepper in Africa, right into the face of poor, old Dr Gerstenmaier. The result was horrifying. Even though we immediately blew out and rinsed his eyes, the burning pain only eased off very slowly. Even today, after so many years, I still feel sorry for the tormented and helplessly wriggling man!

*The mammary glands in elephant cows are situated between the front legs*

## Chapter Twenty-eight

# The Sudan
## The Choir of the Prisoners

My walls at home are decorated with the head of a Nubian ibex from Jebel Kwab Kwab Kumteb, a steep and stony hill amidst the wild and rugged littorals of the Red Sea. This was a memorable trophy and an exciting adventure on which I could write almost half a book. What I would like to narrate from this journey is an occurrence so gruesome and comic that it could never have been invented.

With Mahgoub el Bedawi, my former Mweka student and now the game warden of the Red Sea Province, we drove between Suakin and Tokar. It was such a lonely and dismal area that an American hunter is said to have asked a local: "If you live here permanently – does it hurt?"

Late one Sunday afternoon we stopped at a police station to register as the Sudanese were very suspicious of foreigners. An elderly constable in a neat and clean uniform was on duty and he rang his boss at home who said he would come to stamp my passport.

While waiting for his arrival, Mahgoub and I sat down on a bench in the inner courtyard of the building. On the opposite side, just across a small lawn, was the detention cell which was similar to a large predator cage. Behind the bars, just like in a zoo, some apathetic 'Fuzzy-Wuzzies' – so called because of their wild hairstyle – sat on the ground.

After a while, a woman appeared carrying a tray on her head, no doubt the supper for the prisoners. She handed it over to the constable who started to carry it to the cell when the telephone rang. He put the tray down on the ground and hurried back to his office. He was hardly out of sight when a dozen or so emaciated cats rushed for the unfamiliar and unexpected meal. Instantly, an almost bloodcurdling howl could be heard coming from the cage where the inmates saw themselves being deprived of their food. The cats, fearing that their excursion to the land of milk and honey was endangered, gobbled down the food even more greedily. In the evening twilight we witnessed a scene that could have been borrowed from a medieval horror film.

## Chapter Twenty-nine

# Undeserved Luck

It was in July 1956 that I was hunting not far from Lake Eyasi. Wafts of mist hid the mountain forest with its hanging moss and lianas and the late afternoon was as dark and gloomy as the ebony face of the Mbulu tracker stalking in front of me through the dripping wet tendrils and ferns.

The guide had been recommended to me by Pat Hemingway on the back of whose double-barrelled .470 Nitro Express permit I had purchased a licence to shoot a black rhino, although I preferred to use my trusty 9.3x64 Brenneke even if it was not legal to hunt rhino with this calibre. From the very beginning of my hunting I used only magazine rifles and felt quite confident with my 9.3.

From my first outing I wished I had Pat's heavy double in my hands as, after a short period of tracking in the twilight, an enormous rhino stood in front of us looking as big as a goods wagon. It was the first rhino I had seen outside a zoo and I thought that if I did not place my bullet correctly, it would probably kill me!

What in my inexperience I mistook as impending danger made me act coolly and without any buck fever. My rifle was already steadied on my shooting stick, the sights aimed at the middle of the neck and, at the shot, the monster collapsed on its belly. But what was that behind it? Was it not the twitching of an ear?

I immediately fired a second bullet into my fallen trophy as an insurance shot, whereupon another rhino of the same size rose behind it. The second rhino stood for a moment to gaze about it before starting to move around, angrily snorting and blowing like a railway engine. It stomped several times around its fallen mate while I prayed it would not see us and charge. That would have been all I needed! A rhino shot in self-defence would have got me into real trouble with the authorities but, luckily, we managed to

*My only rhino*

retreat unnoticed and were happy to reach the Land Rover and find our way back to camp just after dark.

As we found out the next morning, my trophy was a big old cow. However, I cannot remember having eaten more delicious meat than the fillet steaks from this rhino, although not having been well hung, they were terribly tough!

To be honest, the hair-raising return up the Ngorongoro Crater wall remains even more in my memory. Unusual rains for this time of the year had made the rough track, with its many flooded gullies, almost impassable. I got stuck several times and, although we were already overloaded, an elderly Maasai stopped me for a lift. My first thought was to decline but I finally agreed with the ulterior motive of having an extra hand to push when necessary. So the old man hopped onto the Land Rover's back but not before placing a magic charm of some crossed blades of grass under a tyre. This was his witchdoctor's medicine to ban more rain. Really, I know I should not be superstitious but soon the low clouds thinned out and we even managed to skid across the black cotton soil of the open plain. It was then a matter of keeping moving otherwise we would have got stuck for days. That awful soil is like soft soap when wet, the dreaded nightmare of all drivers.

In Arusha – shame upon myself – I sold the trophy of my first and only rhino to an Indian for 460 shillings, covering my safari expenses as well as the cost of the licence of 200 shillings. I have forgotten the weight of the horns but the front one measured 26 inches and I could not foresee that, ten years later, the price would have increased tenfold.

I also had to dispose of my trusted 9.3x64 Brenneke, not to serve Mammon but for the simple reason that in Tanzania I was unable to purchase suitable ammunition. In the end I managed to get a box of ten rounds from Messrs. Nazareth, the Lebanese trader in Tabora, but they were of three different bullet weights. I got fed up and sold my faithful companion of my first years in Africa to a very keen young farmer.

As a replacement, I bought a very accurate Mauser rifle from Rupert Luedecke in Nairobi, in 7x64 calibre, with open sights and a beautifully soft trigger pull. To begin with I was highly satisfied with my new purchase but what I could not foresee was that the change could have ended in a disaster. Accompanied by Game Warden Brian Stronach, I shot an enormous eland bull weighing about 800 kilograms with the new weapon. My soft-nose bullet caused the bull to give a high jump and then collapse stone dead after a run of about 60 metres. "That rifle would kill a buffalo too," said Brian. "Why don't you try it?"

Being thus encouraged and somewhat full of high spirits, I very foolishly used it to fire at the biggest of four buffalo bulls, aiming just behind the shoulder. The wounded beast did not leave the small herd which stopped after running about 400 metres. Stalking closer, I was able to recognize the wounded bull, which repeatedly beat at the wound on its shoulder with its horn. After a second shot the group fled, taking their wounded comrade with them.

I became extremely upset and, as I had no solid bullets left for the small rifle, I sent my driver, Selemani, back to camp for my .458. It was late afternoon when, armed with this rifle, we again followed the tracks which led into an evergreen thicket. I sent Nasoro in a wide circle around it to see if the beasts had gone through or were still inside it.

Nasoro returned shortly to say that all four bulls had broken cover right in front of him, one bleeding heavily at the shoulder. We rushed to the spot to find only three tracks in the sand and none with any blood. "Nasoro, what did you see?" I asked but he stuck to his statement and urged me to follow the tracks.

I did not agree, thinking his advice was to dissuade me from

*The one that nearly got me!*

following into the dangerous thicket. I went back on the tracks to where the buffalo entered the thicket and followed a tunnel-like path until it forked. Here we saw a little red speck on a dry leaf. "Here is the last blood," I whispered to Nasoro.

A little further on the visibility was better and I recognized what looked like two, black saplings as the forelegs of the buffalo. Before we could react we heard a snort like a mini-explosion and, the next instant, the bull was on top of us.

I fired an unaimed shot from the hip. The bull showed no reaction and rushed past me at a distance of less than a metre. I heard a scream and the next thing I saw was Nasoro being flung aside as the bull ran over him. I reloaded, turned and ran after the bull, jumping across Nasoro's prone body. Then I was out into the open brachystegia woodland where the bull had stopped. When it saw me it came at me in a full charge. I had time to aim at the charging beast that was coming with its head up. I hit it just underneath the chin, which brought it down and it died while uttering a last, groaning death bellow.

My first and almost blindly fired bullet, I am ashamed to admit, only nicked the dewlap. Nasoro survived with two cracked ribs and some bruises, while Bambala escaped in time. I swore never again to use any light calibre rifle on buffalo.

*Killed at four metres with the 7x64*

But on a Sunday morning only three weeks later, I drove to the Malagarasi to shoot some meat for the kitchen and, stupidly enough, brought only the 7x64. After bagging a topi, I was stopped by some Africans who asked me to shoot a very bad-tempered buffalo bull that had been mauled by lions and was now chasing the women from their watering place.

This, of course, was a demand I really loathed to fulfil but obviously could not decline. On the other hand, I was too lazy to drive the 40 kilometres over bad roads to fetch my .458, especially as I wasn't sure whether the whole issue was a story designed to get some meat. With rather uneasy feelings and only five soft-nose cartridges in the magazine – solid rounds for this calibre were not available – I followed the complainants and was indeed shown the bull's tracks which entered a thicket of high grass about one acre in extent. No way was I going to follow the tracks into that death trap with my light rifle.

I got the men to burn the grass (which was as dry as tinder) and positioned myself at the opposite end of the thicket. With a loud rattling the grass burned very quickly but I decided to give up the hunt and drive home as nothing emerged nor any further tracks were found. I was very thirsty and my water bottle empty, so I asked one of the villagers to take me up-river beyond the settlement for a safe drink.

We had not been on the well-trodden path to the river for very long when my guide almost fell down, turned and ran back. There was the buffalo, standing in the water some 15 metres away, half-facing me. As a soft-nosed bullet would probably have glanced off the head, I fired at the junction between the shoulder and neck, which was partly covered by a horn. After the third fast shot, the bull rose and turned towards me. With no time to think, I fired the fourth bullet at the middle of the head and, as if hit by a sledge-hammer, the beast collapsed. The 11.2 gram H-mantle hollow-point had punched a neat hole through the thick bone of the forehead and penetrated right into the brain. Praise be for RWS ammo!

But what had caused the animal to become so aggressive? There was no sign of a lion attack and, instead, we saw an ugly, festering sore near the pelvic bone in which a spear blade, about five centimetres long, was embedded. It had most probably been fired from a large calibre muzzle-loader from a hide in a tree.

## Chapter Thirty

# THE OKAVANGO
## THE JEWEL OF THE KALAHARI

The professional hunters of Botswana consider a dugout canoe safari, without clients, into the Okavango Delta, a 22 000 square kilometre swampy wilderness with palm wooded islands surrounded by papyrus, to be the closest any of them will get to heaven.

Not quite as romantic, I nevertheless gratefully accepted the opportunity to participate in an ornithological safari in the Okavango, watching from a comfortable houseboat gliding along narrow channels through the endless papyrus which, by the way, is one of the fastest growing plants on earth. The unbelievably rich birdlife made for an unforgettable experience. We were lucky to observe the rare Pel's fishing owl, and were very impressed to see how our young guide attracted the fish eagles to fly down within a few metres of him by holding up a fish in his hand. And of course we saw the swamp's game animals, the red lechwe and the shy and elusive sitatunga.

At night we erected small tents on wooded islands but I preferred to sleep outside on a mattress under a mosquito net. We were 17 in number, all South Africans except me. There were three elderly gentlemen from the Cape who were obviously delighted to be out in the bush and had brought their own wine which they drank after supper while merrily singing the songs of the day. And then, just for me, they sang a song in German: *In München steht ein Hofbräuhaus* (In Munich there is a court brewery).

*The old Ndorobo sat by this fire eating zebra meat*

## Chapter Thirty-one

# In Conclusion

## Timeless Africa

In 1963, while on a college safari in the Tarangire Game Reserve (now a national park) near Arusha in Tanzania, we found rather primitive hides and human footprints so close to a waterhole that we imagined we would have to deal with a very old or almost blind poacher.

Sporadic grass fires also indicated the illegal presence of human beings in the game reserve. One morning a thin pillar of smoke rose above the tops of the trees, so we went to investigate and came upon an old and almost blind Ndorobo roasting some zebra meat in a gully. He was totally flabbergasted by our presence and was apprehended without resistance while claiming to have taken the meat from a lion kill.

*The old Ndorobo*

His possessions consisted of a thin cloth, a bow with poisoned arrows, a knife in a little sheath made from zebra skin and, most interesting to all of us, two pieces of wood with which he was able to produce a flame in a kindling of dry elephant droppings by rotating the one in a small hollow of the other.

He looked very surprised to be seized, obviously quite unaware of any illegal doing and unable to comprehend the meaning of a game reserve in what were the stamping grounds of his whole lifetime. As he did not understand Kiswaheli, we luckily were able to communicate with him through our Kenyan Maasai student, Joshua Orumoi. Our 'prisoner' followed us willingly to our camp, happy and very content to be fed. He was a charming, old fellow and I liked his reaction when some of the students teased the 'wild man' by showing him their comfortable new camp beds we had just received from German Aid and asked, "Have a look at our equipment and then tells us where you sleep at night?" The straightforward answer was simply, "Under the nearest tree when the sun sets."

Although it was against the law, we decided not to hand him over

to the police in Arusha as we were convinced that he would not survive even a day in jail. Instead, our director, Hugh Lamprey, who was a pilot, agreed to fly him in the College's Super Cub into Simanjiro, the next Maasai settlement outside the reserve where he occasionally bartered honey for milk and knife blades.

Completely unafraid and smiling with happiness, he climbed onto the back seat of the little plane, his bow held between his thin legs. His arrival from the air would be the first time ever that a Maasai elder had arrived by plane and he knew the people of Simanjiro would look at him with respect.

*Quo vadis Africa?*
*Africa, where are you going?*

# EPILOGUE

The following joke circulated among the old French colonials. A scorpion wanted to cross the Shari, the Central African river that flowed into Lake Chad. So the scorpion asked a hippo whether it could take him safely over to the other side, whereupon the Hippo answered that it would not take the risk of being stung.

The scorpion said, "You must think I am tired of life? That would be against all reason for then you would drown me!"

Finally, the two agree on the planned crossing but, when they were in the middle of the stream, the scorpion could not resist the temptation and penetrated his poisonous sting deep into the hide of the hippo.

"Are you mad?" cried the hippo. "Now you will have to die."

"But why," asked the scorpion as the hippo dived, which were the last words of the scorpion.

*C'est l'Afrique* – That's Africa!

# TANZANIA

Lake Edward
Masaka
Mbarara
ZAIRE
Kabale
Kagera
Bukoba
Goma
RWANDA
ZIWA MAGHARIBI
Kigali
Lac Kivu
Biharamulo
BURUNDI
Bujumbura
Moyowosi
Malagarasi
Kahama
KIGOMA
Kigoma
Ujiji
Uvinza
Ugalla
Kalemie
Mpanda
ZAIRE
RUKWA
Moba
Rungwa
Lake Tanganyika
Sumbawanga
Mpui
Mbala
ZAMBIA
Kasama